Praise for 40 Voices of Grief ar

"Melissa Jansen's book on grief i
have encountered the life-altering
This book bridges the losses in a way that helps the reader to feel less
alone and to understand that hope in Christ lies beyond even the most
terrifying or heart-wrenching circumstances."

Christa Hardin, MA Relationship Coach and Author, Owner of
Reflections Counseling & Coaching

"Grief is a universal language, but Melissa brought together 40 voices
that declare Hope can be a second language we learn to speak in the
midst of overwhelming loss. Melissa has paired each relatable voice of
sorrow with the undeniable loving voice of the Heavenly Father,
joined them together and ends each encounter with powerful prayers
which speak life, peace, comfort and hope."

Jennifer Reeder, Author of <u>Break the Yolk! From Floundering Flock</u>
<u>to Financial Freedom</u>

"Melissa Jansen has taken some of life's most painful and traumatic
stories and given us hope that resiliency is possible even when we've
faced impossible pain through the incredible power of God's love."

Rita Schulte, Author of <u>Shattered: Finding Hope and Healing Through</u>
<u>the Losses of Life</u>

40 Voices of Grief and Gratitude

By Melissa M. Jansen

Dedication

This book is dedicated to my first love, God. Without Him, I could have never sustained all my losses or experienced the redemption He's mercifully poured on me for over 40 years. This book is truly a book about where His story intersects my story and the stories of those whose voices you've heard.

I would be remiss if I didn't mention that those of you who don't share my Christianity are still encouraged to seek the professional help of a grief counselor or coach, to help you work out your losses. I'd be honored to help you do that if you'd like to connect.

Be blessed!

A Note from the Author

This book has been years in the making. Forty years ago marked my first experience with loss and grief, so 40 is a significant number for me. I've not forgotten the Biblical significance of the number 40, remembering the 40 years that the Israelites spent in the wilderness waiting on the Promised Land, or the 40 long days that Jesus spent in the desert, fasting and dodging temptation and going deeper with his Father.

For many years, I thought I'd write a book about my grief, a sort of testimony, but never felt those losses were worthy of the written page. I wondered if anyone would read it until this past fall, when I felt a nudge that this year was the season to write. I surmised I could be the storyteller of many others' tales of grief and faith.

Next, I received encouragement from friends and family to get writing. Thus, began the process of selecting the 40 "voices" and listening to them as they unveiled their losses – some familiar to me, others a complete surprise. All of them left me in tears but with a sense of peace that I can't explain, other than to tell you that each of their losses was redeemed. I suppose that's because these are the voices of real people, not fictional characters, who graciously shared with me how God carried them through their journey. Because I wanted to retain their authenticity, I didn't undergo the usual process of editing, but tried to capture their heart using the first person point of view. What a privilege it is to tell their story and mine.

This book is divided into several categories of grief: loss of health, loss of job or identity, loss of a friend, loss of a family member including spouse and child, loss of marriage, and loss of innocence. My prayer is that as you read each one, you will relate to either the loss or the person who shared their story. If you are in the midst of grief yourself, I hope these stories will give you some direction for help and hope.

Speaking of gratitude, I wish to acknowledge a few people:

First, I thank my mother, Jane, who was a published author herself and the greatest storyteller I ever knew. Though she won't ever read this, she inspired me to write and I'm forever grateful.

After my mom came my 8th grade English teacher, Miss Anderson, who gave me a love for literature at the ripe age of 13. Though the years and miles separated us, social media brought us back together and she willingly proofread my first draft, forgiving my misuse of punctuation. Miss A and I share an uncanny number of parallels in our lives, including my becoming an English teacher for a short stint, and if you listen closely, you might hear her voice amongst the 40.

Thanks also to my three sisters and my friends in Virginia and Florida. Their positive words and prayers on my behalf have sustained me. I appreciate their patience when I couldn't go for coffee or lunch, or answer my phone because I was strapped in my office chair, writing for hours.

Lastly, a big shout out to my husband and two daughters, who've always supported me in all that I attempt or accomplish. I could not have finished this book, my first, without their encouragement.

Table of Contents

My Story

Without a doubt, no one escapes grief. Grief is part of the cycle of life. For me, many years of trusting God and working with a skilled counselor peeled back the layers of pain. God granted me a second chance at love and marriage, and some wonderful, albeit short, years with my parents. I cherish the special relationships I've shared with those who've passed away. I'm empathetic and passionate about helping people who've lost a loved one, a marriage, or a shattered dream. I'm drawn to them because I've walked the same journey, only in different shoes.

"Something's wrong with Dad, and they've flown him to Walter Reed Hospital for tests. We'll pick you up in an hour," said my sister.

My heart skipped a beat. My mind started racing. This couldn't be happening. "Really, God? Both?"

Two weeks prior, my husband finally confessed what he'd struggled with in our short 22 months of marriage - that he desired to live a homosexual life. Though he loved me, he wanted to separate and divorce so we could go on with our lives. He knew I wanted children and he told me I should marry again. He wanted to spare me the pain but was too late. I'd already committed myself to the marriage and to being a military wife, both of which were shattered in one day.

Hearing the news of my father being ill felt like a second punch in the stomach. My sister and I met my mother at the hospital and learned that Dad's x-rays showed two brain tumors. We were all stunned. He was only 52, after all, and at the top of his military career. He'd served 32 years in the Army including two tours in Vietnam, and was a four-star general. My mother and he were planning their retirement in Florida, and were very much in love. We believed his pending surgery and treatment would save him. My two older sisters joined us and the four of us girls strategized about how we could best support our mom. My marriage was in crisis and I was in the middle of directing a spring play. I crumbled. Once again, I didn't understand God's plan.

No stranger to losses, I recalled my first love dying in a motorcycle accident, at age 16. Just 14 myself and madly in love, I gave my heart and a promise of the future to him. We planned to go to college in Florida together after graduation and marry after that. Though we were young, we spent all our time together, until my father got his orders.

Raised in the military, I moved every two or three years but I never got used to it. Moving out of state, going to a new high school, leaving all my friends and my sweet boyfriend, Mark, was brutal. One month after we moved to Georgia, on an early Saturday morning, I received a phone call which jolted me from my sleep. My mother handed me the phone. As I heard my sister's boyfriend on the other end, I gripped the handle tightly and closed my eyes as his words sank in.

"Melissa, I have some bad news. Last night after a party, Mark was riding his motorcycle and he hit a parked train. He didn't make it. He's gone."

I screamed, but nothing came out of my mouth. In shock, I collapsed to the floor, dropping the phone. My parents ran into my room. The rest was a blur.

Eventually, I called my best friend, who'd been at the party the night before. I asked her if someone identified his body, and she said his best friend had. I called Mark's sister, who was on vacation with her parents in Chicago. My parents helped me with the travel plans to the funeral. I went to church that Sunday, but I couldn't pray. Everything felt surreal, like an out-of-body experience. My body functioned like a robot, but my heart was broken. My heart was empty, with no room for anyone else.

Once I arrived in Chicago, I went to the funeral home for the visitation. With an open casket, Mark reminded me of a wax figure, though he was as handsome as ever. I wondered if I could ever love anyone like him again. That's the day I began using my defensive coping mechanism: putting up walls as an emotional barrier for pain.

Throughout the next few years of high school, I used alcohol and drugs to block my pain. I went on dates occasionally but maintained caution about relationships. In the back of my mind, I feared losing everyone I cared for and pushed them away. I continued on a self-destructive track, using anything I could to suppress my pain. I hit rock bottom, until one night when I found the perfect man: Jesus. I surrendered my heart and learned to trust again.

During my college years, my parents were still on the military fast track and stationed in Germany. They arranged for me to visit during my summer and winter breaks, and I adored traveling in Europe. During the summer of 1981, I agreed to go on a blind date with a young lieutenant named Bruce. His commander worked for my dad and invited both of us to his home. As we talked over dinner, we learned we shared much in common such as our choice in music and fathers who were both in the Army. That summer we shared a great courtship, going to festivals, military dances, and church together. My parents liked him and his parents adored me. We agreed our relationship was growing with each visit.

Though separated by many miles when I returned to college, Bruce and I corresponded monthly by letters and saw each other on my breaks. The relationship was magical, all I'd ever wanted. However, shortly before my graduation, he came to visit me for a few days. His demeanor was more reserved than I remembered. Something had changed but I couldn't put my finger on it. After he left, I broke off our romance so I could clear my head and date other guys. As the months passed, Bruce began to write letters again and one day he called to ask if he could see me that Christmas. Both of our parents were living in Virginia, near each other, so I agreed to see him.

My parents had invited both Bruce and his parents to their party on that icy December eve. The weather created an impossibility of driving home, so we talked for hours while sipping champagne. At one point, Bruce said he didn't want to be friends anymore. I thought that sounded strange, but he followed it by saying he wanted to be my husband. Though I told him I would consider his proposal and he could change his mind in the morning, he declined. He wanted an answer. Knowing I loved him, I said yes.

After spending the night in the guest room, the next morning Bruce asked my parents if he could marry me, and with their blessing, we planned the wedding. Since both families were military, our wedding was held in a beautiful historical chapel, with a regalia of soldiers with swords, and a horse-drawn carriage. We spent a peaceful, sun-filled honeymoon in Florida, and I was content. By July, we left for our first assignment in Arizona.

For six months as newlyweds, we made friends with other military couples. We rented a small adobe home and adopted a basset hound puppy. My career as a full-time teacher was on hold due to our short assignment, but I substituted at the local high school and taught fitness classes. By Christmas, we knew that our next assignment was Washington, DC for at least one year. Thrilled to be closer to his parents, we moved cross country, bought a home, and settled in.

I secured a full-time teaching job while Bruce worked long hours at the Pentagon. After one year, he seemed distracted and agitated, which reminded me of his behavior during the college visit. Curious about what was bothering him, I asked him but he changed the subject or told me he was stressed. By that spring, something was awry.

After a week-long spring break vacation with my girlfriends, I returned to an emotionally distant husband I didn't recognize. He didn't kiss me or physically connect in any way. I wondered if he was sick. After a few long days and nights of not communicating, he returned home in a blissful state. He transparently told me that he was equally attracted to men and women. He told me he'd struggled with his sexuality in high school and college, and his parents sent him for counseling. As an intelligence officer in the military, concealing his secret lifestyle was imperative. My mind was racing but my body froze. Stunned, I ran into the bathroom for a silent primal scream.

Two weeks later, with my marriage in crisis, my father was dying. Dad sweetly asked each of my sisters if he needed to ask our forgiveness for anything before he went into surgery. My dad was a great protector and great provider, so all I wanted him to do was hold me and comfort me. At that moment, I realized I couldn't lean on either of the two most important men in my life, the two whom I loved the most.

I cried out to God, "Why, Lord? Why me? Why do you keep taking the men I love away from me?"

At the time, without much theology behind me, none of my losses made sense. Though I felt secure about my salvation, I wondered if I was being punished for some sin I'd committed. I wanted answers. I wanted to die. Perhaps dying was easier than carrying on alone. I had to support myself financially, deal with the possibility that I was infected with HIV, give up my dream of starting a family, and try to move forward.

Paralyzed some days, I got out of bed, went to work, and supported myself. Mercifully, my health was protected. Several months later, my father died. With no other choice, I accepted losing both men. Many years passed before I accepted that God didn't "take away" the loves of my life. He allowed the circumstances. He taught me along the way that I'd made idols out of my boyfriend, my father and my husband. Graciously, He protected and provided for me.

Though I never expected to, along the way, I met a wonderful man and married again. Despite that huge blessing, I brought some baggage with me into the marriage. I carried a lack of trust and a fear of abandonment. I feared that all my wonderful blessings might end in catastrophe. Unfortunately, that is a side effect of traumatic grief.

Thankfully, 30 years later, I am convinced more than ever that my purpose here on this planet is to comfort others with the same mercy and grace that was granted to me. My story intersected with God's story and He re-wrote mine. What was intended to hurt me and bring pain was transformed by a loving God, who gets all the credit and the glory for healing me.

Grief & Gratitude

"Praise be to the God and Father of our Lord Jesus Christ, the Father of compassion and the God of all comfort, who comforts us in all our troubles, so that we can comfort those in any trouble with the comfort we ourselves receive from God." (2 Corinthians 1:3,4)

Prayer: My Lord, I could never have imagined my life without You. Through all my losses and all my trials, You have been faithful and merciful to me. You comforted me like no other could, and You have given me a gift of mercy so that I can comfort others who are hurting. I am forever grateful that You are on the throne - past, present and future.

Billy

"Where am I? What happened to me?"

When I realized I was alive, I was still confused as to why I was lying in a hospital bed with tubes inserted in me. I wondered why I wasn't at my football practice.

Seven years ago, while teaching my second period history class, I fell onto the floor in mid-sentence. My co-teacher called an ambulance and the next thing I remembered was lying in the emergency room while someone injected medicine into my groin. I learned later this was to break up the clot in my brain. I was only 49.

The next few weeks were foggy but because of my stroke, I camped out in a few different hospitals. After several weeks of rehab including physical therapy, occupational therapy, speech therapy and psychiatric evaluation, my doctor told me I had to retire from 26 years of teaching and coaching. Because I loved my students and my football team, I was devastated.

My loving and supportive wife Nancy jumped into action. Understandably, she was overly anxious about my condition and prognosis, but she drove me to all my appointments and she still does. Many of our friends and family prayed for me after the stroke and throughout my recovery. In addition to my stroke, I developed diabetes and a heart condition, which prevented me from any electrical stimulation to my paralyzed arm and weak legs. I was just grateful to be alive.

I never experienced any of the normal emotions after a stroke like anger or depression. I'm not able to drive myself anymore, which is frustrating because I see so many crazy drivers out there. One of my arms is paralyzed and I'm limited at times. However, I can still do one thing I love. I sing in the church choir and I'm very blessed to do that. Though my body doesn't do what I wish, my voice still works.

Music is my pathway to God. I may not be able to quote a Bible verse or tell you the scripture reference, but when I hear my pastor give a sermon or speak from the Bible, I say, "I know a song about that!"

As a Christian, I know God is alive and knows everything but when you are young and dumb, you don't know that. Through the experience of my stroke, I realized He was merciful and wasn't ready for me yet. He still had a purpose for me. Now, when I pray I don't ask for specific things but I ask that God does with me what He wants.

How can I complain? Retired now, I sleep when I want, get up when I want, and do whatever I want. It's not so bad to wake up and see beautiful palm trees outside. In fact, it's kind of what I imagine Heaven is like. Now that's a blessing!

Grief & Gratitude

"Shout for joy to the Lord, all the earth. Worship the Lord with gladness; come before him with joyful songs" (Psalm 100:1,2)

Prayer: Lord, I am grateful that though my body may not cooperate, I can use my voice to praise You through songs and worship. Be glorified in that each day.

Tonya

"Legally blind? Really?"

I couldn't believe my ears, or the diagnosis the doctor gave me. After seven eye surgeries and a detached retina, the doctor told me I'd lost my peripheral vision. No longer able to drive long distances and no longer able to work, I wondered what my identity would be now.

As a child, I was severely nearsighted by age nine and I wore coke bottle glasses. By age 27, I wore 5.0 contact lenses and 3.75 magnifying readers. By age 49, I went on disability which was very disappointing, considering I'd gone to medical assistant school and graduated with honors. While my new medical assistant position gave me purpose each day, that was short-lived.

I don't go anywhere these days except Walmart occasionally, since I can only drive a short distance and never in the rain. I stay home with my mother who's survived three strokes and has dementia. It's like living with a two-year-old. It's certainly not what I'd have chosen, but my life is not over.

Raised in a military family, I moved a lot and once I graduated from high school, I married and gave birth to two great children. My daughter, my greatest cheerleader, now lives close to me and my son blessed me with a grandchild. Sadly, my two marriages didn't last and I moved home with my mother, 12 years ago. I went from being a housewife to a student to a medical assistant before my health declined. Some days are better than others, but I've never blamed God or anyone else for my troubles.

At a young age, I was close to my grandma and we went to church together. When I chose God as my Savior, I put my trust in Him for everything and never cursed Him. I may be legally blind but I believe He still has a purpose for me. My purpose now, even with my disability and the inability to go to work, is to take care of my mother. That's my full-time "job" for this season of life. It's tough some days taking care of Mom when my eyes burn or run, but I'm grateful for little things like my sunglasses.

Sometimes I bump into things when I'm trying to help my mom and I have the bruises and bumps to prove it! Sometimes I'm sad because no one is expecting me to show up at work or follow a schedule, but I'm grateful that I've still got my mother, my kids, and good people around me for support. We're moving to a newly renovated house very soon and I couldn't be happier.

Every day, even without healthy eyes, I focus on God's grace and mercy. One day in Heaven, I know I'll have a perfect body and perfect vision. That gives me tremendous hope.

Grief & Gratitude

"He will wipe every tear from their eyes. There will be no more death or mourning or crying or pain, for the old order of things has passed away" (Revelation 21:4)

Prayer: Lord, You know how I struggle with my health. Some days are better than others. In the big scheme of things, I have no right to complain. I am so grateful for how You carry me and lead me and the promise of no more tears one day.

Kathy

"Can I help you? Can I pray for you?"

"Yes, please, my husband is up in surgery," I responded.

This wasn't the first of Greg's surgeries. During college, in 1980, he survived his first surgery for Crohn's disease. He's 57 now, with four subsequent surgeries, and he lives each day as if he's got intestinal flu. Most adults have over 20 feet of intestines. Greg only has four feet left. Three of his six siblings, a nephew, and our oldest son have suffered from this disease, which has certainly left a dark cloud over us throughout the years. I wouldn't wish this condition on anyone. Facing surgeries with complications and infections is a risk, not to mention daily struggles with eating. With a feeding tube, which goes directly into his vein, Greg doesn't complain. He could've claimed disability 30 years ago, but still goes like the Energizer bunny! I believe he's been given an extra dose of grace.

Thinking back on that day in the hospital chapel, I so appreciated the eucharistic minister who'd offered to pray. We're Catholic and I'd just sadly learned that Pope John Paul II passed away. After the minister and I prayed, I walked upstairs to Greg's room in the ICU and saw a poster on the wall. The poster was from the movie "Miracle on 42nd Street." Elated, I realized that the hospital we were in was located on 42nd Street in Lincoln, Nebraska, and we'd just come through a miracle. Greg would survive and his recovery from this surgery was the most rapid of all his previous ones.

During one of Greg's other surgeries, I sat in the waiting room and noticed a small book called *The Word Among Us*. It's a monthly devotional and this one contained an article about God's timing. That little article spoke to me directly, in the sense of knowing that if Greg were to be healed, that would be in God's way and timing. I'm in favor of prayer and healing services, but I'm also reminded that we don't get everything we want in this life. This can be a daily struggle even for believers.

Someone with a disease like Crohn's may be tempted to give up, and a spouse who is married to someone with a chronic disease may get discouraged or leave. I never even considered it. When I took my marriage vows, they included sickness and health. They meant until death separated us. Though at times it's been very scary and I've been concerned about provision for our family, God's been faithful.

Greg and I both imagine what our lives might've been like if he didn't have Crohn's. We see healthy couples walking hand in hand and are reminded of all our blessings. Would he like an unencumbered life, free from the bondage of disease? Of course. However, we both believe his body will be whole one day in Heaven. I'm grateful when that day comes, Greg won't have any more pain and suffering. My oldest son won't either. Finally, the dark cloud that's hung over us will disappear and we will rejoice.

Grief & Gratitude

"My comfort in my suffering is this: Your promise preserves my life." (Psalm 119:50)

Prayer: Dear Lord, sometimes the pain and suffering are unbearable. In those times, I thank You for your promises of comfort and of eternal life in Heaven, where our bodies will be whole and we'll endure no more pain.

S tan

"Honey, I think you need to come in here. Right now!"

In March of 2014, the day before my birthday, I was home working on some gaslight lamps with my wife. I went inside our house briefly to grab something for the project, and my eyeballs went nuts. My right arm shook like crazy and I couldn't understand what was happening. I knew I'd lost control, which wasn't good. I yelled for my wife.

"Oh my God, what's the matter with you?" she asked.

Colleen took one look at me and called 9-1-1. She convinced me to sit down, and we waited about 20 minutes for the ambulance to arrive. I now know you have a three-hour window after a stroke in which a medical team must inject a shot to break up the clot. Thankfully, the EMT's worked quickly. After my initial emergency room visit, I transferred from that hospital to another one, to be treated by a neurologist. Following that treatment, I spent 21 days in a rehabilitation hospital. My brain didn't swell, fortunately. God's hand was protecting me.

On the day of my stroke, I woke up in the hospital and realized my eyesight was severely affected. It's been the same ever since. Three quarters of the field vision in my left eye and one quarter in my right eye is gone. I've been told that because the stroke affected the left part of my brain, my sight is the only thing damaged along with some minor balance issues. I've got no speech or swallowing problems. For about eight months, I endured physical and occupational therapy, striving to regain some strength. Working toward the ability to drive, I took every possible test on my field vision. Unfortunately, I failed those tests and can't legally drive, although I go about one mile to the commuter parking lot.

You see, driving used to be my lifeline. As an outside salesman for a food distribution company, I drove for a living. I drove hundreds of miles for work and even more on our vacations. After my stroke, being unable to drive forced my resignation. I accepted a new job selling insurance, and my wife and two daughters drove me when I needed to meet with a client. I tried to claim disability but the government denied it, saying I could still walk and talk and could, therefore, work.

I was nervous, with four kids to support, so I cashed in part of my IRA. I finally found a company who hired me to do entry-level inside sales work. The job allowed me to sit in an office and I've done that ever since. At 55, it's hard but I'm grateful to work and bring home a paycheck. I rely on two women who meet me at the commuter lot and drive me to and from work each day. One drives like a NASCAR driver, and one rides her brakes constantly. Yes, their driving tests my patience, but I know the Lord has a sense of humor.

Speaking of the Lord, I wasn't raised in a Christian home. I don't remember my parents taking us to church ever, but when I met my wife at 20 years old, I joined her and her family at church. My mom is now "religious" and my dad told me he prayed for me after my stroke. Truly, I know God saved me from dying, especially when I learned how many people suffer fatal strokes. I have heart disease and I've gone to a cardiologist since I was 30, but I guess I never expected to suffer a stroke. At times, I get angry because I can't drive freely like I used to. Maybe I'm a little envious of others. I confessed that to a priest one time and he reminded me how merciful God is. After my stroke, I began to thank Him for my wife and children and for the many blessings I've been given. I'm so grateful for my ability to keep working and providing for my family, and I know without a doubt God touched me. Like the apostle Paul, my "thorn" is a small detriment. I can still persevere and I can minister to others who've suffered a stroke.

Grief & Gratitude

"But He said to me, "My grace is sufficient for you, for my power is made perfect in weakness. "Therefore, I will boast all the more gladly about my weaknesses, so that Christ's power may rest on me." (2 Corinthians 12:9)

Prayer: Dear Lord, forgive me when I complain about my weaknesses or physical disabilities. I am so grateful that You saved me by grace and extended your mercy to me time and time again. Help me be bold and tell others about You and what You have done.

nn

"Mom, what's wrong with you? You're scaring me."

"Go get Dad," I responded.

The truth was, I wasn't sure what was wrong. My heart was pounding, I was pale, and I felt like a dark cloud hovered over me. I was lying in bed with my daughter reading when everything came apart. I asked my husband and daughter to pray for me but nothing changed. Within minutes, they called an ambulance and we went to the hospital.

The doctors ran tests, said nothing was wrong other than anxiety, and sent me home. They offered me medication, which I declined. Further, I was losing weight fast – I'd gone from 120 to 89 pounds and felt awful. Every day, I stayed in bed, sleeping for hours, and insisted on keeping the drapes in the house drawn. I felt so downtrodden. As a Christian, I cried out to God when I couldn't find the strength to read my Bible or pray. I was in a dark place. I didn't realize I was suffering from clinical depression.

Perhaps the depression was triggered by the death of my father, six months earlier. Perhaps because I carried too much activity on my plate. Perhaps because I felt I needed to be everyone's caretaker. Sadly, I took care of everyone except myself.

My mother passed away in 2010. When I was young, I believe she suffered from depression because she slept for hours during the day. She also struggled with menopause, although she didn't share that with me until years later. Prior to her death, my husband and I took care of her because my dad struggled with his own health problems. We drove both parents to two different rehab facilities, while trying to raise and home school our daughters, run a business and manage many volunteer ministry activities. I'm a nurturing person, so my nature wasn't to "check out."

My healing took three years and at times, I didn't get up out of bed or shower because I felt too weak. If friends came by to visit, I told my husband, "Don't let them in." At one point, some of my family members thought of committing me to a psychiatric hospital.

Instead of traditional hospitalization with medication and therapy, I chose alternatives. By using natural herbs and supplements and changing my diet, I started to heal. Throughout my journey, I leaned on the Lord for strength and answers, and I clung to the scripture *I will never leave you or forsake you. (Hebrews 13:5)*

I remember a defining moment when my daughter, now married, called and said, "Mom, please don't hurt yourself. I love you." At that moment, I believed the Holy Spirit was counseling me. He was telling me God wasn't finished using me. Years later, I still believe that admonishment.

Over the years, I've wondered how many people prayed for me. I've marveled how my husband could've been so patient with me. I've reflected on my depression and I've been curious about what contributed to it. Since my childhood was chaotic and my mother suffered from depression, I've wondered about a generational curse. Since ours was a dysfunctional home, and I was the "caretaker" for my siblings and parents, I've thought that's what put me over the edge. I've entertained the notion that hormonal factors affected me and my suicidal thoughts resulted from trying to juggle too many things. I'm saddened that some people carry a stigma of shame toward those with depression.

Even though I didn't choose traditional medicine or mental health counseling, I never stopped focusing on my mind. My goal was a sound mind, so I worked on renewing my mind and thoughts daily. By allowing my mind and heart to be transformed, God healed me. Each day, He gave me purpose and strength for another day to live.

Each morning, before I step out of bed I thank Him. I realize I wasn't created by myself to be alone but created for His purposes. He is directing my life, which means He gets to decide my destiny, not the other way around. I encourage others who are depressed to examine their lives and get the help they need, with any method that works for them. I tell them to rest assured, as I did, that God will never leave them or forsake them.

Grief & Gratitude

"Those the Lord has rescued will return. They will enter Zion with singing; everlasting joy will crown their heads. Gladness and joy will overtake them, and sorrow and sighing will flee away." (Isaiah 35:10)

Prayer: Lord, You truly did rescue me and made me whole again. While I was once sad and depressed, You lifted my head and crowned me with a new joy. Thank You for being the lifter of my head and the lover of my soul.

Melanie

"Someone prayed you into this meeting," the speaker said.

A lightbulb went off. Yes, someone surely did that for me, since I couldn't pray myself. I was attending an Alcoholics Anonymous meeting during my second stint in rehab. Getting sober the first time failed, but this time I knew my drinking must stop. I literally couldn't take another drink, fearing what it would do to me. One more drink would certainly kill me.

I'd been an occasional drinker for most of my adult life. At 47, I found myself in an unhappy marriage with a desperately ill daughter. Lonely and menopausal, I was confused. I found myself wanting to "check out," and drinking numbed my pain temporarily. I "buzzed" through my days to cope with the chaos in my mind. My alcohol addiction crept up on me, leaving me in a choke hold before I realized what was happening.

Due to having a sleep disorder, I'm only awake during the day with the help of medication. I got to the point where I would wake up, take my meds, and crave alcohol. I'd spend the rest of each day drinking, adding vodka to iced tea, diet soda, fruit juice or anything to disguise what I was doing. I was good at fooling everyone except myself.

My childhood was tough, split between two parents. One was physically and verbally abusive, and the other very loving. I never felt abandoned or forsaken, yet a pervasive sense of being broken plagued me. I believed in God, went to church, and attended Bible study in college. After having my daughter, I taught Sunday school and VBS. Once I was addicted to alcohol, I stopped going to church, stopped praying, and lost my connection with God. When I finally hit the rock bottom point of wanting to end my life, I honestly believed "someone prayed me in" to rehab.

At 52, when my drinking peaked, my husband confronted me. I fought him and continued to hide my alcohol. Sneaking around was exhausting! Finally, with my marriage severely damaged, I agreed to my first stint of rehab. I left for Georgia.

Our insurance only allowed for a maximum of seven days, so afterward, I went to live with my brother and his family. I stayed sober for two months, but I started to drink again to drown out all the uncertainty in my life. I hosted my own two-year pity party. I cooked, cleaned and helped my brother with his kids, hiding my drinking. Rarely sober, I was so depressed. Sometimes I went for a week without taking a shower or brushing my teeth. Living in daily fear, I became obsessed with dying and contemplated suicide.

I knew I needed to detox again, but not without a bang! I sat in the parking lot of the rehab facility, completely drunk, before I checked myself into the program. The doctor, an addiction specialist, told me I needed rest. He gave me a shot and I slept for two solid days. I know the staff gave me medication for symptoms of withdrawal and monitored my vital signs. However, I don't remember much else.

After three days of rest, I determined to live my life again. Since my sleep disorder medication is addictive, they couldn't administer any during treatment. I constantly struggled to stay awake during therapy and class meetings. Even though I've got a master's degree in counseling, I knew little of the complexities of addiction. I forced myself to stay awake, knowing I needed to learn what they needed to teach me. The doctor tried several different medications to deal with my sleep disorder, without much success.

On my scheduled day to leave, I suffered a severe reaction to my new medication. My doctor fought my insurance company to give me additional time in the program. Unable to even sit up in bed, I could barely move and evidently experienced some sort of psychotic break. Perhaps a spiritual break, because for the first time in many years, I prayed.

I cried out to God, "Please take away whatever is happening to me!"

After being told that my insurance company agreed to pay for 10 additional days of treatment, I spent two or three days watching my body return to normal. I stayed in treatment a total of 17 days. I finally felt some relief. I felt healed.

Sober for 18 months, I've been reunited with my husband and daughter in Virginia. I'm still learning I can have fun without drinking, and I must stay away from certain friends and situations which could trigger my drinking again. I guard my sobriety closely. I won't jeopardize staying clean for anything. I'm terrified of addiction so fear keeps me sober. I've got an immense amount of love and support from my family and friends, and now I rely on my reestablished connection with God.

I realize God truly had a purpose for me and that includes being healthy and whole again. He didn't want me to die. I understand He saved my life and gave me strength exactly when I needed it. All I did was ask and have faith that He would answer. Finally, after so many years of chaos, I feel peace.

Grief & Gratitude

"He lifted me out of the slimy pit, out of the mud and mire; he set my feet on a rock and gave me a firm place to stand." (Psalm 40:2)

Prayer: Lord, I would still be at the bottom of the pit if not for You. Thank You that someone prayed for me, and thank You that you loved me enough to save me in spite of myself. I am forever grateful.

Gayle and Kimberly

"You need to move out. You're an addict and you need immediate help," I told my daughter.

Gayle: My journey with my daughter's heroin addiction led me to God. Her subsequent healing is evidence that He loves her more than I ever could. No matter how deep my love for her was and is, only God could extend unconditional love, mercy and grace to her. Through her road to sobriety, and my own struggles with coping, I witnessed how God saved her life and saved both of us in the process.

I wasn't raised in a Christian family, and my husband wasn't either. Once our two children were born, church and God were ambivalent, and we never made them a priority. Our daughter, Kimberly, was an introverted teen and strived to fit in well. Her anxiety, much like mine, caused her to struggle in social situations and by age 15, she rebelled.

Kimberly: I was drawn to people my age who were different. By that I mean weird, and as a teen, I identified with others who shaved or colored their hair, or wore multiple piercings. I linked up with people who used drugs because I felt those people understood me.

In 9th grade, I met my first boyfriend. We skipped school together and began using heroin. After my first experience, my brother told my parents and they immediately shipped me off to a rehab program in Louisiana. During this stint, I met others who were actual drug addicts and I felt like I'd made friends with whom I could identify. Because I struggled with anxiety, I believed drugs would help ease the difficulty of social settings. Sadly, drugs only led me to a dark path.

Gayle: Once Kimberly returned from rehab, we watched her closely. We tried to be supportive but noticed her slipping more and more as she stayed with her boyfriend. Little did we know, she started injecting heroin and other opiates. She was good at hiding it, while working as a medical assistant and completing her GED. Because of her addiction by age 17, we insisted she move out of our home.

Kimberly: I moved in with my boyfriend at the time, while his dad paid our rent. We lived in a bad place with no power or water at times. We woke up every day and hunted for drugs. We even stole clothing from stores, so we could re-sell them and buy drugs. This lasted for 5 years, until my boyfriend was arrested and went to jail.

While he was incarcerated, I hung out with the wrong people and continued using. I went to a party, met a guy for a hook-up, and became pregnant. While he wanted nothing to do with the baby, I never considered not having my child and asked my parents for help. They agreed to help me rent an apartment near them, and were very supportive when I delivered my son in 2006. Life was good. When I worked full-time, my mom would keep the baby. Eventually, the baby's father came around and decided he wanted to be involved. We moved in together and became a family.

At three months pregnant with our second son, we got married. I didn't crave drugs and loved being a mother. One day, the doorbell rang and my husband was served papers for child support. Apparently, he'd fathered twins about the same time he'd fathered our first son. I was devastated. To make things worse, I found bags of pot in our medicine cabinet, and realized he was selling and using drugs again. I reached out to my family.

Gayle: We were concerned about Kimberly and her husband, as well as the children. They moved to New Hampshire for a job opportunity, which was very far from home. While they liked the area, she was isolated with no car when her husband went to work, with very little support for her two toddlers. She felt completely alone when she discovered her husband was having an affair with a co-worker. I drove up and got her and the boys, and we headed back to Florida. We made room for them all in our home, and began to attend church. My son's girlfriend invited us to come, which was perfect timing as I felt desperate. One day I sat on my lanai and prayed, "God, if you will save my daughter and son, and my family, I'm all yours."

Kimberly: During my darkest days, I prayed to God for help and deliverance. My marriage was in crisis and when things got bad, I ran to drugs. My parents spent hundreds of dollars on lawyers and supported me any way they could. I felt stuck.

I reconciled with my husband and he took a job in Fort Myers. We lived in an apartment complex with unsavory people and I was drawn, once again, to drugs. I felt like a horrible person and a terrible mother. While my children were at school, I would get high and still manage to function. Eventually, this destroyed my marriage and led to losing temporary custody of my sons. We separated and my husband was understandably concerned. One day, in court, the judge told me I was unstable and to bring my kids to live with their dad. Afraid to tell my boys that they were going to live with him, I tried to carry on.

Gayle: I helped Kimberly fight for partial custody, which was granted to her after three weeks. Her husband agreed to move closer to us, and we helped Kimberly get sobriety treatment. She entered a methadone clinic, and eventually broke free from all the drugs. We helped with the kids while she went to nursing school. God was making a way. We began to go to church, and were baptized together.

Kimberly: I'd dreamed of going to nursing school and once even blew the chance when a doctor I worked for offered to pay for it. Now, finally sober, I worked hard and graduated as a registered nurse. Finally, I was free from the addiction of opiates and no longer identified with addicts. Truly, God changed me, giving me a new identity. This new path allowed me to work with patients in a hospital and now I'm on the other side. Though my co-worker and patients aren't aware of my past, I've got greater empathy because of my journey. Though I still don't like crowds or certain social settings, I experience less anxiety. I'm grateful to God for my new life.

Gayle: I remember at one point, lying on my couch immobile, thinking my daughter is a drug addict, my husband is drinking heavily, and I have a teenage son who smokes pot. I didn't know how we got to that point or what to do about it. Thankfully, my mother-in- law challenged me, telling me to stop wallowing in self-pity so I attended Al-Anon. I learned about boundaries and that I couldn't "fix" anyone. They made their choices and could choose whether to get help. I've learned not to judge people, including my family, and I've learned that I can cast all my cares on God, who loves me unconditionally.

Grief & Gratitude

"So do not fear, for I am with you; do not be dismayed, for I am your God. I will strengthen you and help you; I will uphold you with my righteous right hand." (Isaiah 41:10)

"Do not be anxious about anything, but in every situation, by prayer and petition, with thanksgiving, present your requests to God. And the peace of God, which transcends all understanding, will guard your hearts and your minds in Christ Jesus." (Philippians 4:6,7)

Prayer: God, only You can deliver us from our anxieties and from our addictions. All You ask us to do is surrender and call upon your name. Thank You, God, for carrying me through my dark journey and never leaving me. Thank You for rescuing me from the valley of death and putting me on the right path. Thank You for your unconditional love.

P~aul~

"Are you ready for this?" my wife asked.

"I think I am. I'm tired of the cold weather and I'm tired of the traffic. Let's do it," I replied.

I wasn't completely sure, but time was ticking. Both kids were on their own and weren't coming back to Virginia. I'd worked for 37 years and anticipated something new. A new home, new climate, new freedom, and new purpose. Nobody ever prepares you for retirement and all that it brings. One day you're going to an office from nine to five and have a safety net of superiors and subordinates. The next day, you're solo. Once you retire, you think you've lost your identity and, sometimes, purpose.

I've never allowed things I did professionally to define me. My faith in God and my values extended into my daily life and choices. They transcended the things I did, including work. I grew up with loving parents, and after college and some soul-searching, placed my faith in Christ and His teachings. With a successful career, first in teaching and later in administration and local government, I worked with kids. The opportunity to impact them and be impacted by them was phenomenal. Later, as a parent, I experienced first-hand what patience and persistence meant in my own role modeling. My core principles stayed intact but my purpose changed.

Though God gifted me with certain talents, I possess an impulsive mentality at times. I want certain things right now. Two and a half years after retiring, I'm still searching for some clarity about what I should be doing on a volunteer basis. Not unlike Biblical characters, my life is not orderly all the time nor do I see God's purpose instantly. Collectively, we all go through seasons of life knowing that when one chapter ends, another one begins.

So, what's a typical day like now?

Before retirement, my day depended on external factors. Problem-solving was what I liked because the solutions were usually rewarding. I now joke about "time" being relative to internal factors, such as how long I want to sleep in, whether I want to go to the gym or swim, or the weather forecast. I'm not pushed or pulled by a boss or a community. I choose what I want to do and when I want to do it. I've got very few restrictions. However, even with some freedom and no expectations, I'm tempted to drift off into my comfort zone, without ever finding purpose.

Recognizing I'm no longer 25, and with fewer career and volunteer opportunities at my age, fear and anxiety creep in. However, through prayer and conversations with my wife, we lay a foundation for our future and we find exciting new things to explore each week.

For me, prayer is important for finding purpose. Prayer for me is an on-going conversation with God, with no starting or stopping point. Since retirement, I've prayed and found three important ways to serve as a volunteer – one with children, one with guide dogs, and one with my wife in ministry. All three are rewarding and use my gifts. Each involve a certain "identity" although I know my identity is in Christ. It's important to remember that God hasn't changed – He's the same yesterday, today and tomorrow and He's the same whatever season of life you are in.

Grief & Gratitude

"Have I not commanded you? Be strong and courageous. Do not be afraid; do not be discouraged, for the Lord *your God will be with you wherever you go." (Joshua 1:9)*

Prayer: Father, thank You for leading me and providing for me, wherever I go. Help me to trust You even when I'm in a new or strange place, knowing You are right beside me.

Sarah

"We've decided to move in a new direction."

"So, in other words, I'm terminated," I responded, still not believing I heard her clearly.

Two weeks after receiving a huge award from the national church organization, and a great year of international awards, my work came to a grinding halt. All my dreams shattered. After seven years of devoted leadership and a 32-year career, the end came down to a complaint filed against me and a new leader's decision. I called my family before the press got ahold of them.

I took a long walk before I shared the news with my spouse. Clearly, this was a politically driven decision and a vindictive way of "cleaning house." We sat down to dinner and blessed the food, as was our custom, and thanked God for our many blessings.

Memories of Mom flooded my mind. A pillar of southern charm, Mom was nurturing, protective, and "present" for us. She was a champion for my siblings and me, no matter the cause, ever-joyful and aware of how hard being a preacher's kid was. In private, our parents allowed us to form our own opinions and challenge theology. Deeply knowledgeable about scripture, Mom used the Bible as a tool for learning, not for rebuking. We never questioned her love.

I wondered how Mom would've reacted to my sudden loss of employment and the decision of the ministry. Since I couldn't talk to her anymore, I chose to be gentle with myself, only using gentle words. No "stupid" phrases about what I may have done. I attended a gentle yoga class. I listened to Christmas carols. I thought about 2015, when Mom was dying. When she passed, I couldn't breathe without her. At times, I'd curl up in the fetal position and try to find air. Over time, I remembered the same God that created my "supermom" cared for me. He understood my emotions. Choosing to embrace all the gifts he'd given me, I stepped forward to maneuver this change in my life.

Before Mom died, her prayer life was fierce. With a cabinet full of gift mugs from people she knew, they served as reminders for her to pray for each of them every morning. Though I don't have as many, I go through the same ritual now. As I hold each mug, I pray for each of my loved ones and those I serve.

Before she died, Mom wanted a full manicure and pedicure. She walked on a beach in Galveston even though she felt miserable. She wanted her kids and grandkids – all 26 of us –surrounding her and we did. Gratefully, she was confident in knowing her Lord and Savior. It was difficult as I sadly watched my father, 86, with his own illness and grief, and watched how my siblings each reacted. After Mom died, I went back to my parents' Asheville home, which she designed and decorated. I sat in her favorite chair and felt her presence. When I visited their church, I felt such pain but let the tears flow.

Now, with the loss of my wonderful job, I gave myself permission to cry once again. Having been a chaplain and working in ministry for so many years, I understood grief. Like others, I suffered through all the stages. Shock. Anger. Weeping. I did what Mom would have done: Prayed. Gave thanks. Accepted. Moved on.

Grief & Gratitude

"Therefore, since we are surrounded by such a great cloud of witnesses, let us throw off everything that hinders and the sin that so easily entangles. And let us run with perseverance the race marked out for us, fixing our eyes on Jesus, the pioneer and perfecter of faith. For the joy set before him he endured the cross, scorning its shame, and sat down at the right hand of the throne of God. Consider him who endured such opposition from sinners, so that you will not grow weary and lose heart." (Hebrews 12:1-3)

Prayer: Gracious and loving Lord, I thank You for teaching me to let go and be gentle with myself. When everything around me doesn't make sense, I am grateful that You bring meaning. Thank You for the lessons I have learned. Thank You that these trials are temporary. Thank You that You don't grow weary even when I do.

Sylvia

"What did I do wrong, Lord? What am I going to do now?"

I was soul-searching, talking to God, and couldn't express myself fully. I was dying without dying. The pain and rejection were overwhelming and I felt severely depressed. I felt so isolated after stepping away from the ministry and my husband was worse. He'd slipped into a cave, spiritually, and wasn't coming out anytime soon. I considered divorce and spoke with a lawyer. I begged him to go to counseling with me. Finally, I realized our marriage was not the problem. While divorce was the easy way out, that was not the solution, so I didn't give up on him. More importantly, God never gave up on me.

I met my husband in my late 30's, in my home country. A widower, he was 10 years older than me and an established pastor. When we married, we considered having children since my biological clock was ticking, but decided instead to throw ourselves 100% into ministry. As a team, we hoped to build our church and the kingdom of God. From the beginning, we didn't separate home life and ministry. I led the worship and counseling services, while he preached. We skipped vacations altogether. Called to minister to our flock as well as street people, we provided food and assistance to many, including Muslim women. Our church grew from 400 to 2,000 within two years.

Over time, because we preached fundamental biblical truths, a rebellion arose. During the 1980's in Europe, a liberal spirit of darkness prevailed. A large group of radical Islamic terrorists formed in our region and we started a revival. My husband boldly preached against their beliefs and their brutal acts, while some of the members of our church (including leadership) came against us. The tithes we'd depended on to minister dwindled and eventually ended. Sadly, the church was taken from us. The members, once part of our flock, weren't willing to pay the price of being a fundamental Christian. Consequently, we didn't fight and left the country.

When we came to America and settled in Florida, a pastor who became ill passed the baton to my husband. Again, we built the church by training leaders and developing the ministry. As outsiders, we found difficulty in building trust with the church members and eventually they also rebelled against us. They made accusations that we were "control freaks" and too "radical" in our sermons about extreme Islamic elements of terrorism. Some of them broke into our offices and stole from us. The church collapsed.

At that time, I became emotionally distraught and unbalanced. I experienced great physical stress including allergies, insomnia, and heart problems. Thankfully, by working with a holistic nutritionist and changing my lifestyle, I felt better. Still, I questioned, "What will I do now?"

Temporarily separated from my husband, I discovered I loved working with dogs. I trained for my certification, while my husband physically and emotionally stayed unavailable to me. He eventually agreed to some counseling and slowly started to work his way out of the spiritual cave in which he lived. Due to a heart issue, he suffered a minor stroke and I believe this softened his heart. Likewise, my work with the dogs gave me a new sense of purpose and peace. Able to step back from the pain and rejection and hear from God again, I felt His cleansing. My husband and I moved to a new place and started our lives over again.

We still remember the hatred and persecution we endured and now we're cautious about our relationships. Perhaps the ministry was an idol for us. Perhaps God used us for a season. I believe if I went back into ministry, I'd do many things differently. I still need more healing. However, I'm grateful to God for never leaving us, and for pruning us as we went through the fire. I'm so grateful for the new, sweet relationship I have with my husband. That, alone, is a miraculous work of God.

Grief & Gratitude

"Dear children, keep yourselves from idols." (1 John 5:21)

Prayer: Holy God, I am so grateful that when we take a wrong path, You come alongside us and correct our course. Thank You for guiding me and bringing me back to You. Thank You for restoring me and for restoring my marriage. Thank You for giving me a new passion.

Danielle

"You've got to be the man of the house now, son."

"Okay, Mommy, I can do that," he responded.

Just nine years old at the time and the only other male in the family, my son wasn't ready to take on the burden of leading and protecting our family. My husband George, a National Guard soldier, was preparing for his first deployment. I didn't understand all of what that entailed, but I soon learned what being a single mom in charge of a family was like. We threw things together quickly, unsure of where George was going or when we'd see him again.

George is seven years my senior. At 14, mature for my age but quite shy, George was my school girl crush. He worked with my uncles and we played pool together every Sunday. As our dating progressed, our romance blossomed and we got engaged during my junior year of high school. George's childhood was rotten, so my parents adopted him into our family right away. Because of my free spirit and uncertainty, I broke our relationship off until years later at my great-grandfather's funeral. I saw him again and not long after, we got together and I became pregnant. However, I still didn't commit fully to George.

During this period, I'd moved further away from my childhood faith in God. Raised in a liturgical denomination, I rebelled but I believed God was there. Toward the end of my pregnancy, I started praying again and received an epiphany about our family and our future. Though we'd separated, God led us back together.

In 1990, after the birth of our first child, George's unit was deployed to Operation Desert Storm. We married shortly before his deployment and lived with my parents off and on for financial support. Upon his return, George was assigned to a homeland unit, about an hour away, but we only saw him rarely on weekends. By 1998, the National Guard wasn't focused on retention, so George left to work for a landscaper for three years. His work hours were long and hard but it helped us rebuild our security. On September 11, 2001, everything changed.

George stopped by the recruitment office and signed back up.

I screamed, "What about our family? Don't you care about us?"

He explained because he wanted to protect us, not harm or hurt us, he was going. Though a young bride and mother, I dove right in. I headed up the Family Readiness Group for his unit and made some decisions for the first time. Since George deployed in October, we had a very short window to set up direct deposits for our bank account and get our military medical insurance set up. Additionally, our youngest daughter was very anxious and ill with stomach issues. With our country in turmoil, and with terrorism at its highest, I learned to advocate for myself and family. I'm a bit of a loud mouth. One day, I marched up to the unit headquarters and told the colonel our bank account wasn't active yet and the mortgage was due. He personally wrote a check, for which I was grateful.

However, single parenting wasn't easy. I was still required to participate in school activities, cook and clean, and couldn't really communicate very often with George. He couldn't come home and "fix" things as he wanted to, and I didn't want to burden him. In those days, we didn't have social media and ways of communicating like we do today, so I'd limit how much information I shared with him.

Six months later, George's unit deployed again, to Guantanamo Bay. While much of his life was on hold, mine changed dramatically. Our kids became teens, our daughter was still very sick, and when he came home on leave, I treated him like a stranger. I'd say things like, "Don't talk to them like that." Because I'd established some parenting standards, I didn't want him to change them. One time when he was gone, a mouse got into the kitchen and I was terrified. Leaving the house in a hurry, I left some dishes in the sink. When George came home and saw the dirty dishes, he was mad and admonished me. That's the moment I knew we needed help.

During his deployment, I came out of my shy shell and made many friends. I loved my new social life, with having the freedom to go where I wanted, when I wanted. Unfortunately, I couldn't pick up the phone and share with him the details or the trials of my week. We were distant, physically and emotionally. I was close to divorce. Deep down, I knew we were meant to be together and I fought to work things out. I'm so glad I did. When George came home, we realized we were both committed to staying together but we needed to set some new boundaries. When he found full-time work, and felt better about himself, we grew as a couple. We put our marriage above everything else.

Through 20 years of marriage, I still felt I was lacking something. I didn't have a relationship with God and neither did George. We both wanted more. After searching, we found a church we both loved and got involved with. That's when we began to pray about and work towards a new dream.

For 20 years, we'd told friends and family about our dream to move to Florida. We spent many vacations at Disney World and loved the warm climate, so when our daughter went to college in Tampa, we took a trip to hunt around. Sooner than anticipated, God led us to the perfect neighborhood and perfect home, and He made a way for me to relocate my real estate business. Meanwhile, seven years from retirement, George shared our dream with his National Guard leaders and was told he could join me in Florida within a few months. Sadly, when the time came, they said, "Sorry, it's not going to happen." Our dream of starting our new life together was shattered.

Currently, we're still separated by many miles. Though not by deployment, it's still difficult to be apart. We are very intentional about our visits, which are no more than two months apart, and we talk every day by phone. I have my parents and youngest daughter with me, while George has our other daughter, son, and grandchild near him. My business is flourishing and I've made new friendships. Many people question how this works for a husband and wife.

The difference between deployment and our separation this time is it's our choice, not one the military or someone else made for us. Additionally, we trust God with our marriage and know that He's ultimately in control of our dream. When I first moved away, I prayed God would bring my husband to Florida and provide a new job for him as soon as possible. However, I realize God is doing something much bigger, financially and spiritually. His way and His timing is different than ours. I trust that He's led us to where we are now and He'll continue to lead us. Our marriage is stronger than ever and we're making new memories. We don't sugar coat things when they're challenging, but work as a team and anticipate the day when we'll be in the same home. We know the military prepared us for our current separation for a season, but we cherish our future together, trusting God for everything.

Grief & Gratitude

"For I know the plans I have for you," declares the Lord, *"plans to prosper you and not to harm you, plans to give you hope and a future." (Jeremiah 29:11)*

Prayer: God, thank You. I am so very grateful to You for the healing in my marriage and family. Our plans are not often your plans. Thank You, Lord, for the new hope and the future You have freely given us.

Andy

"Having troubles readjusting to life in Belgium?"

As I stared at the bulletin board, the flyer caught my eye. With an invitation to a meeting, I was intrigued. What perfect timing.

The day of the meeting, I arrived early. I saw no one. I went into the assigned room, sat in a chair and waited. Finally, a beautiful woman dressed in a sari walked in. She reminded me of an angel.

"Are you here for the meeting for people having trouble adjusting to life in Belgium?" I asked.

She said, "Yes, I'm Bali and I'm leading the meeting."

"Where is everyone else?" I asked.

"Well, I've been coming for four years and you are the first and only person who has ever shown up."

Bali explained that many women in Brussels couldn't admit that they were alone or having difficulty. She told me she was thrilled I came. She shut the door and I burst into tears. She could see I was lonely and scared, so she took my hands in hers.

She asked, "Are you a Christian?"

"Well, I'm Catholic," I responded.

"No, I mean, do you know Christ? Is He your friend?"

I didn't know what she was talking about. I didn't really know Jesus. I only knew of Him. Once I got married and converted to Catholicism, a priest and a lay person taught me everything about the Catholic faith and I'd never studied the Bible. I didn't feel I was worthy or qualified. Though I was a competent person and academically bright, I knew absolutely nothing about the Bible. As a former Jew, I knew rabbis could spend 50 years studying one verse of the Torah! I was 43 and knew nothing.

Bali took my hand and said, "You're coming with me to Bible study. I'll pick you up."

She picked me up for the next four years. She was my mentor and my tutor and introduced me to other smart, funny and gracious women. They were missionaries from the UK, Ireland, Scotland, Germany and Belgium. We formed an undeniable bond. Later, Bali and I opened a counseling center which ministered to senior citizens. I learned so much from her about the Bible and more importantly, about Jesus.

Several months before that first meeting, my husband came home and dropped a bomb.

"We're moving to Belgium," he said.

"Wait, what? When? How did this happen?" I was stunned.

He said, "I interviewed for and accepted a position with Hughes Aircraft. I'm leaving in a month. You can wait until school gets out in June, when you and the girls can join me in Brussels."

Several years prior, Eric worked for several years for companies in Washington, D.C. but Europe was a huge change. I realize couples today are more likely to discuss major changes before such hasty decisions, especially one involving a move overseas. Eric made the choice before we'd discussed anything.

At 42, I was working full time and raising a 10 and 13-year-old. They were just getting used to the idea of their father traveling six months a year, plus their hormones were out of whack. Other than my co-workers and a few friends in Virginia, I knew no one. Furthermore, I didn't speak French or Flemish. I felt overwhelmed.

I, alone, was responsible for renting the house, selling the cars, packing all our belongings into three separate shipments, and wrapping up loose ends before moving to a foreign country I knew nothing about. I didn't have a cell phone or a computer with internet access at the time. The only move I'd ever made was from Denver to D.C. after we were married. I was 19 at the time.

As a young Jewish girl, I left my abusive home to marry the man I'd fallen in love with in college. I converted to Catholicism although I knew very little about religion or God. Though we were cultural Jews, my parents only celebrated Passover and Hanukkah. My siblings and I were physically and verbally beaten down and I couldn't wait to escape. Eric was my ticket out of Hell. Handsome and bright, he was quite successful and I'd follow him anywhere.

Now, sitting in my kitchen with my yellow pages and a phone, I wasn't so sure. How was I going to survive? Back then, no one could tell me anything about Belgium, and the company Eric worked for was so small and had no one on staff overseas to help guide us. Later we discovered many other working Americans with larger companies and lawyers negotiated larger salaries, better benefits and additional help. We weren't as fortunate.

Meanwhile, my daughters were excited about moving and getting to see their dad more often. After finding renters for our home and selling our cars, we stayed in a hotel for an extended time until school ended. We anxiously purchased our plane tickets and planned to leave in mid-June. While waiting, I went for all my medical check-ups, not knowing what kind of medical care we'd have in Europe. After one appointment including a mammogram, I received a call with the news about a lump in my breast. Following a biopsy, I would need to wait for my results.

"What do you mean, I have to wait?" I asked.

"Well, one of the technicians thinks the lump could be cancerous and another believes it's benign. We'd like to send off a biopsy for a pathology report, which will take six to eight weeks."

"Seriously? I'm moving to Europe soon and I don't have time to wait."

Because I didn't want to go to a foreign country without answers, I waited. For eight long weeks, I was terrified and considered all my options. The girls and I sat in a hotel room during a brutally hot summer with nothing more than our suitcases. Finally, by August, I got the call I was waiting for. My pathology results for cancer were negative and I was free to go. Unfortunately, my mood dampened during those long weeks and I was hesitant. Still, I was grateful I would get to see Eric again and we could start our new life.

Off to Brussels we went, and after our initial reunion, we settled in. While the girls were in school all day, I was stranded at home, isolated with no car and no friends. Two weeks later, Eric announced, "I have to go on a business trip."

Since we were stationed in Europe, I thought a business trip might mean to the U.K. Instead, Eric was going to market the aircraft in the Far East. I protested, telling him he couldn't leave. With no bank account, no car, no job, no friends, and no command of the language, I was scared. He managed to transfer some money to a local bank four blocks from our house, but he left me without a car or computer. We had a telephone but long distance calls were very expensive, which prevented me from staying in touch with my siblings and friends back home. Thankfully, I brought an electric typewriter and we had a fax machine, so occasionally I would type letters and fax them to my friends for support.

Since I didn't have a car, I had to walk everywhere including the grocery store and bank. I didn't know any of my neighbors since most spoke Dutch, German or French and were very territorial. Eventually I discovered a great deli and a wonderful chocolate shop a few blocks away. Belgian chocolate soon became my best friend, which was evident by the fifty pounds I gained before returning to the states. Clearly, I was lonely.

When Eric came home, I insisted I needed a car so we bought an old VW Golf, though I was terrified of driving in Belgium. Fast, crazy drivers were everywhere, not to mention filling up cost nearly $75! Since employment was out of the question for American women, I talked to others about volunteering but they told me Belgium was a socialist country with no such thing. I decided to pursue a master's degree but my husband had to bring my textbooks from England because we had no access to military libraries or the internet.

Through my daughters, I heard of an American Women's Club. The idea of a social club was fun and exciting, and a means to meet other women from the U.S. Little did I know, the women were all about status and very judgmental. I related to none of them and sank into a deep depression.

Finally, one day I went to the club by myself and I saw something that grabbed my attention. On the bulletin board was a flyer with an invitation to a meeting for people who'd had trouble adjusting to life overseas. Though a risk, I thought I had nothing to lose. I'm so glad I risked going because that day my life changed forever.

After meeting Bali and forming a bond with the women in the Bible study, I had a revelation about my purpose for coming to Europe. A former Jewish girl who strived for perfectionism because of my childhood, I was proud and lost. Literally taken from my home and the comfort of America and dropped into what I perceived as the pit of Hell, I found my purpose. When I got there, you know who was waiting for me? The only One I could hold onto and trust. Finally, I experienced love with no more abandonment. Finally, I felt true grace.

Recently, I thought about my life and how I once wanted to be a doctor so I could save lives. I wondered why God allowed me to live in a home with abusive parents. I wondered where I could've been, and where I thought I should've been. Next I thought, "How do I know I haven't saved a life?"

Because someone took my hand when I was lost and helped me, I wanted to do the same. Once I trusted Jesus, I wanted to share Him with everyone. When I returned to the U.S., I volunteered with many ministries where I could do that. I met many foreign women, afraid and lonely or oppressed, and I told them I understood. I knew what it's like to be alone and afraid. I knew what it's like to be rejected. More importantly, I told them about the love of my life, and how He rescued me from the pit of Hell, and how He longed to do the same for them.

After many years and many miles on the journey to bring me to my knees, I know now that I didn't lose my identity. Gratefully, I gained a new one.

Grief & Gratitude

"Though my father and mother forsake me, the Lord will receive me."
(Psalm 27:10)

Prayer: Father, I am so grateful to You for adopting me as your daughter. Thank You for pulling me out of an abusive home and calling me your own. Thank You that while I tried to find my identity in jobs or places, I came up empty. Thank You for taking me halfway across the world and dropping me there, so that I could meet my true identity: my identity in Christ.

Phyllis

"Mom is preparing to die now. She isn't eating so this might be a good time to visit and say your goodbye."

Gayle's daughter called to give me the news. I flew out to visit with half of the group for a final visit.

Our "group" consisted of 10, all bridge players who met in 1978 in Kansas. I'd moved from Philadelphia with my husband and was recovering from a hysterectomy, so game nights were an opportune time to make new friends. Some of the ladies were veteran bridge players, others not so much. More than cards, we talked about our troubles, trials and families. Bridge nights were a nice girls' night out, and one of my newfound friends was Gayle. Our group continued to meet until my career took me out of Kansas, in 1991.

Since we were all busy and separated by miles, we didn't reconnect until 2005, when one of the ladies suggested an annual reunion trip, with different destinations each year. Our group members lived in Kansas, Colorado, Texas and Florida. When our reunions started, we named them "therapy sessions" because they gave us each a chance to talk about our successes and failures, and share stories of our children and grandchildren.

During one reunion, about four years ago, Gayle sadly told us she had pancreatic cancer. She said she'd felt like she had the flu, but her eyes were oddly yellowed. By the time she went for medical tests, the cancer was advanced. She chose to do a seven-hour procedure, during which they removed most of her internal organs, cleaned out the cancer, and put her back together. Since we were unsure of her prognosis, we pushed up our next reunion to the spring – this time in Charleston, South Carolina.

Gayle joined us in Charleston in May, but she was fragile. Weak and wasting away, she ingested 17 enzyme caps before each meal.

Preparing ourselves for her inevitable demise, we mourned, although she and her husband spoke positively about experimental treatments. By fall, I received the call from Gayle's daughter.

Half our group flew out to be with her, but I made mine a quick trip because honestly, one day was enough for me to say all I needed to say to her. I wanted to remember the good times with the healthy Gayle – the fun times driving her Corvette, the parties, and the bridge group reunions. I had to let go and allow Gayle to go.

About three weeks later, I tried to call Gayle again. Her daughter said she was too weak to speak and the end was near. While I was in Lake Tahoe that Christmas, Gayle passed away. I didn't go to her funeral but grieved for her in my own way, crying on my daughter-in-law's shoulder, and writing Gayle's name in the sand.

What's kept me strong in the loss of my dear friend, and with the passing of other loved ones, is an understanding of the cycle of life and death. I believe in God's will. Naturally a guarded person, as I've matured, I've learned we must go through a mourning process. There's no pill to take the pain away. Time heals for some. When I grieve, I drain myself of sadness and God returns me to gladness.

God's will and timing are perfect. As painful as death is, God understands because He sacrificed His son for us. By that act, I know I'm forgiven of my sins and I have no expectations of my mortality. I know God numbers all of our days.

Grief and Gratitude

"There is a time for everything, and a season for every activity under the heavens: a time to be born and a time to die." (Ecclesiastes 3:1-2a)

Prayer: Heavenly Father, we don't know how many years we have on this earth. Our lives are like a vapor. People whom we love come and go, and we are full of sorrow. Help us in those times to remember that we have the promise of eternity in You.

T om

"Death. Are you ready?"

Those four words rang in my head and heart for many years after I heard them. When a priest I knew spoke them, my reaction was and still is this: If you're not ready, what are you doing to prepare?

Throughout my life and my career, I've met some people who are faith-filled and sure of their destiny. Likewise, I've witnessed some who aren't. Thankfully, I was raised in a Christian home with parents who taught us about God and service, and modeled that daily. I do think faith is a gift and it's up to us to receive faith daily. Moreover, when faced with a loss or setback, I'm convinced that people without faith can't navigate grief or make any sense of their circumstances. Thankfully, I leaned on God when we lost Doug.

When I was assigned to the national office in Dallas, Doug was my staff leader. He was a tough guy from New England but was fair and thorough in his leadership. In my 27th year with my organization, I received a lousy evaluation from Doug. In fact, I was given the worst possible review. Normally when that happens, an employee is given 30-60 days to improve his performance or face termination. At the time, my wife and I had financial obligations and commitments, which didn't afford us the freedom to start over or relocate.

I'd witnessed a colleague of mine, who'd just completed two weeks of leadership training, get terminated. After my own evaluation, I walked out of Doug's office and told another co-worker what'd happened and sensing my shock, he offered to teach my class. I declined and told him I needed to teach the class myself so I could improve my skills. Still, I circled back with Doug on my review, worked on a performance improvement plan, and invested heavily in getting to know what his frustrations and expectations of me were. All this time, I leaned daily on God and He was my source of strength.

Over time, my relationship with Doug grew and I learned that he'd fought cancer off and on for a few years, but each time he bounced back. Once our national office made the decision to reorganize and when Doug failed to get promoted, he retired fully. However, he took time after his retirement to call each staff member at home on Thanksgiving, reminding us that he still cared for us. That really touched me.

Sadly, two months later, Doug passed away. I was angry at myself for not reaching out more after he left. After we got the news, I was asked to make some calls to let others know of his death. I took a deep breath, said a prayer, and did that. Unfortunately, I couldn't go to his funeral in New England. To this day, I'm not sure of Doug's faith because we never talked that intimately about it, which is another regret I have. Even though at one point he and I had an adversarial relationship, I learned much from him. More importantly, I learned through the process of that poor review that life's disappointments are not all about me.

One of the lessons I've learned is that we don't go through this life alone. Sometimes we rely on others to help us or teach us. We don't get what *we* want all the time. It's important to ask God what *HE* wants for us rather than what we want. We must die to ourselves to be born again, and Christ offers us that path. From there, it's up to us to keep our focus in the right place, paying attention to mistakes we've made and to correct them. In moments of loss or temporary setbacks, we merely need to accept redirection and accept what's most important. Doug offered that feedback to me and God offers that to each of us. We just need to be His witnesses and share the good news with others.

Grief & Gratitude

"Whoever acknowledges me before others, I will also acknowledge before my Father in heaven." (Matthew 10:32)

Prayer: Heavenly Father, thank You for being my comfort, no matter my trial. I am extremely grateful for opportunities to learn and for those who lead me. Thank You for being my ultimate teacher and advocate. Help me to acknowledge You to those in my path, and to those who don't yet know You.

Mary

"Mary, I'm just not myself. Something's not right."

"Well, you need to get to the doctor now, before the holidays creep up on us."

That was three days before Thanksgiving and unbeknownst to me, only three weeks before my dear friend of 33 years passed away. By the following Sunday, she called me from the hospital to let me know they'd run some tests and were waiting to find out what was causing her pain. Sadly, the medical team couldn't determine until after my friend passed that she had a very rare form of bone cancer, which rapidly attacked all of her red blood cells.

To say I was in shock is an understatement. You see, this tiny little woman, close as a sister to me, was my spiritual compass for three decades. I questioned my own faith and how to apply prayer when I finally grasped this news.

In 1983, when we first met, she walked into the office and said, "I'm brand new to this job."

I replied, "Well, that's good because I'm brand new too!"

Over the years, though so very different in many ways, we worked together. At times, she supervised me, at times we were peers, and at times I supervised her. That never affected our friendship or our trust in each other. Very unassuming, she didn't sparkle in a crowd. While I moved at a very fast pace, she would take her time. She'd joke with me, saying things like, "If you would just slow down, we can talk this through." I'd reply with, "Well, if you'd just hurry up we could get some things done!" We laughed and cried and shared many personal things, good and bad.

My dear friend's tragic past was filled with so many obstacles, but her deep loyal faith in God never waned. She readily told other people about Him and how He'd carried her through everything, and she was undoubtedly the most faithful person I've ever met. She invited people to her church and gave a word of encouragement to anyone she met. I was astounded at how peaceful she was during her last weeks in the hospital, reaching out those who visited her. I stood in a corner of her room one day and marveled at how selflessly she prayed for others. Stunned, I realized I didn't have that kind of faith.

Truly, watching my friend in action was the catalyst for digging deep inside myself. I needed to search myself and ask God for some understanding. Was I angry? Yes, I was. At 65, I felt this woman was cheated. I didn't want God to take her yet, with a husband, children and grandchildren who needed her. Even after her retirement from full-time work, she came to where I worked, as a devoted volunteer.

Inevitably, when nothing could be done to heal my dear, tiny friend, her family asked if she wanted to go to hospice or go home. She said, "I want to go home."

Once she was home, a few of us went over every day to visit and surrounded her with flowers, candles and music. I'm not so sure she even knew we were present. You see, I believe that she was already transitioning to go "home" and she knew exactly where home was! She had no fear. She had total peace which resulted from her devout Bible reading, prayer times, and her relationship with the Lord.

When my sweet life-long friend went home to Heaven, I was asked to give a eulogy for her celebration of life service. To be honest, I don't ever have trouble communicating and anyone who knows me will attest to that, but that day was different. I kept my head down and read my notes, so I could keep my composure. As I witnessed a packed church, I saw a sea of faces, people to whom she had ministered. Besides her own family, friends from church, former colleagues, and others who volunteered with her at a foster home organization, were there. Again, I was amazed. I shouldn't have been surprised, knowing how many friendships she'd nurtured over the years and the multitude of lives she'd touched. In fact, I used this quote when I gave her eulogy:

"Blessed, so blessed are the women who share a lifetime of tears and laughter, for they shall be known as sisters." (author unknown). The truth was, I was closer to this woman than my own sisters.

After her service, I returned to work. I saw the spot where my friend and I used to drink our morning coffee, talk through our issues, and sometimes pray together. I felt a huge void. After six months of disbelief that she wasn't walking through those doors again, I reluctantly accepted that I couldn't pick up the phone and call her anymore.

Thankfully, the nature of my job gives me the opportunity to get out of myself and give back to others daily. After many months, I slowly began to accept that my sweet prayer partner was at peace. She was in the presence of God, whom she loved so much. Oh, how I wanted that peace! That marked the beginning of my own spiritual growth, with the same faith that she exhibited in her life. For that, I'm eternally grateful.

Grief & Gratitude

"Do nothing out of selfish ambition or vain conceit. Rather, in humility value others above yourselves, not looking to your own interests but each of you to the interests of the others." (Philippians 2:3,4)

Prayer: Father, I desire to be humble and to live a sacrificial life. Remove from me my selfish ways and fill me up with more of You. Amen.

Maggie

"Do you know my daughter, Margaret Ann? You resemble her so much."

"Yes, I do. Mom, I *am* Margaret Ann."

I don't go by that name anymore, but I still call my mother Mom. That was my saddest memory to date, since her frail body and mind succumbed to dementia and old age. Over 90 years old now, I stare at Mom and I'm staring into a mirror. She named me after herself and with that came an inherited sense of strength, compassion and nurturing. Recently, Mom and I shared a sweet moment when I crawled into bed with her early one morning. I patted her on her belly and asked how in the world I ever fit into her tummy. We both laughed so hard.

Life with Mom wasn't so full of laughter in the early years. In fact, my relationship with her was very tense. Somewhere along the way, Mom reminded me that as a baby, I was colicky and cried for weeks. Years later in therapy, my counselor and I surmised that my first expressions from Mom were frustration and anxiety, as she held me tensely. However, going through my infant scrapbook, those perceptions were far from accurate.

Later, as a teen in the late 60's and early 70's, I craved a social life and one way of meeting friends was through our church youth group. Leading us was a very hip priest who asked us to call him by his first name, Mark. When I talked to Mom about him, I referred to him as "Father Mark." She was quick to correct me, admonishing me to call him by his reverent name, Father Glasgow. When I was eager to go to a conference in Steubenville, West Virginia, which had a reputation as a city full of brothels and bad behavior, that trip was out of the question by Mom's standards. Frustrated, I couldn't make any sense of her decision.

One night, a nice young man I was interested in came over wearing a nice shirt but a ponytail and sandals. Judging by Mom's glare, that did not sit well. If a friend of mine was of another race, I could forget it, she didn't approve. I hated going to the country club for dinner, where all the members were white and wealthy, while the wait staff were African American. When I talked with my dad about it, because I felt closer to him, he told me, "That's just the way things are. Your mother was raised by strict German parents. Don't expect her to change how she views things."

As I matured, things didn't change much. When Mom came to visit me in college, I broke out in hives because I was afraid of all the things she wouldn't approve of or find out about. Smoking, drinking, and boys who visited dorm rooms weren't high on her list. After college, I lived with my parents for a while and wasn't allowed to go out after seven. If I wanted to go with friends for pizza at 10 pm, I left by seven, stayed with a friend for three hours, and finally got pizza so I'd be home by midnight.

If Mom thought I was gaining weight, she'd give me Weight Watchers cookbooks which created body shame in me. The night before my wedding, instead of talking with my mother, I conferred with my aunt, who supported me and told me to marry the man I chose and loved. I'm convinced we missed some important moments and memories together.

As I've aged, and as Mom's gotten elderly and lost a great deal of her memory, I've realized my relationship with her has changed for the better. We've transitioned, her first being my adversary and later, my advisor. I've realized so much of her well-intentioned guidance was for my best interest. When I sought a divorce, Mom loaned me money, and after a few payments, she forgave the rest of the debt.

Years later, during her visits, we'd cook and sew together, go to church together, share family memories and laugh a lot. After sharing with her about my new relationship, Mom acknowledged that God put him, along with his special-needs son, in my life so that I experienced that nurturing spirit. Instead of dreading visits and perceived criticism, I yearned to see Mom and hear her soothing words.

These days her words are caring and loving. Although her memories are absent, my mother and I laugh together. Though I grieve the loss of her memory and her health, I thank God for healing Mom in a different way. He's changed her. She's softer now and I view her differently. The struggles we've had resulted in good memories. They've been part of the fabric of my life and I'm stronger for them. In a way, our roles have reversed and now we're making new memories.

Grief & Gratitude

"Gracious words are a honeycomb, sweet to the soul and healing to the bones". (Proverbs 16:24)

Prayer: Dear Lord, though we can't choose our family of origin, thank You for placing us in them and teaching us how to love one another. I am so grateful for the years You've given me with mine and the healing that has been granted.

Craig

"Son, I'm so sorry. She didn't make it."

Those words were surreal. Just minutes before, I'd received a call from my dad telling me that my 28-year-old cousin was in trouble. Five days after giving birth to her second child, she'd contracted a fever and fell ill. Despite the medical team's attempts to resuscitate her three times, she didn't respond. Due to a mix-up with her blood test results, they didn't know she'd tested positive for Strep B. Unfortunately, during prenatal testing, her lab results were switched with another pregnant woman's results, and she was never treated. Within 20 minutes, she passed away.

Still in shock, I clung to my break room chair at work, still trying to make sense of something so senseless. When my supervisor came in and realized something was wrong, I told him I just wanted to be alone. I vaguely remember telling a co-worker later that he needed to cherish every moment of life because we're never sure of how long we have. My cousin lived such a short life and I wasn't sure at all what good, if any, could come of a young mother who left a husband and two young children behind.

My cousin and I, just two months apart in age, spent many hours together at our grandparent's house. Because she didn't have the most stable upbringing, they reached out and basically raised her. We hung out often when we were young and even later when we drifted apart, we stayed on each other's radar. When she got married and moved to Texas, I went out for her wedding. Then I got married and had kids. Both of us were living our dreams.

Six years later, I couldn't understand how or why her life was cut short. Still, I knew I'd go to her funeral and pay my respects, which was difficult for me because I don't like viewings or open caskets. The shell of someone's body doesn't bring me any closure. However, I said my farewell at her gravesite and then we headed back to her home for a family gathering.

My first time seeing my cousin's baby was at her home, during the reception. I felt so strange watching my grandma, the woman who'd helped raise my cousin, holding her great-grandchild. The memories of our childhood came rushing back. Wiping away tears, I struggled with accepting that she was gone. To this day, I still can't bring myself to delete my cousin from my phone contacts. There's something soothing about seeing her name on my phone and on her Facebook account. I'm not ready to let go. As of now, her husband remains single and is raising their daughters alone.

I don't understand God's role in allowing my cousin's death, but I realize I don't have to understand. I just have to believe that God is in control and my cousin is in a better place. I've led a sheltered life while my cousin had a challenging one, but I know she's at peace now. Without God, all of this would be senseless and I still question what good can come of two young girls who've lost their mom. However, it's made me take stock of my own life and what matters to me. As a therapist, perhaps I will be more prepared to counsel clients who are struggling with losses and minister to those who grieve. I'm reminded that everything under Heaven happens for a reason.

Grief & Gratitude

"My soul is weary with sorrow; strengthen me according to your word." (Psalm 119:28)

Prayer: God, when I don't understand why bad or sad things that happen, I cling to You. I don't have to know the why's all the time, but I am grateful that You have all the answers. All I must do is search your Word when I am weak and weary and I find comfort. Thank You for your sovereignty.

T ory

"What do you think Heaven is like?" he asked me.

"Oh God, give me the right words," I prayed.

My brother Ed, four years my senior and my sweet protector, was dying. Though raised in the Catholic faith, we never talked about deep things like Heaven and I wanted to be sure I gave an accurate, biblical answer.

I said, "Well, from what I've heard, it's an amazing place. It's the ultimate paradise, and whatever makes you joyful here on earth will be magnified in Heaven ten times."

He didn't say much after that, and not until he was hallucinating and dying from starvation did we surround his bed and pray. We said The Lord's Prayer, and I privately prayed that he'd see Heaven sooner than later.

My brother dealt with stomach issues for years. He wasn't a good eater and had intestinal surgery before, but we were shocked when we learned of his pancreatic cancer. Upon hearing his diagnosis, he went to several doctors who gave him and all our family hope. He had surgery to remove the full pancreas, his gall bladder and part of the intestines, which made him very weak.

Ed was a bachelor and lived alone, so I went to stay with him in New York as often as I could over the course of eight months. That equaled half a dozen times. I'd stay one or two weeks at a time, feeding Ed and taking him to doctor appointments. While I was trying to encourage him, I found myself angry.

I was angry at the medical team. Something just wasn't right. After Ed's surgery, they told us he no longer had the cancer, and he'd be okay if he ate. He got worse. Basically, because my brother had no appetite and wouldn't eat much, he was weak and dying of starvation. I thought, "How in the world does that happen in America? I'm sure something should be done, like giving him a feeding tube."

Ed started hallucinating and one night while he thrashed, the medical staff tied his hands to his bed. He said, "They are treating me like a monkey." My heart was broken.

Though not a man of many words, Ed knew enough to recognize he might not survive. After he passed, I kept asking myself if I could have done something to help him. I wondered if I'd been a strong enough advocate. After all, he'd been my big brother and protector for so many years, and I couldn't pay him back.

The following Friday night, the medical team gave Ed a feeding tube so he wouldn't starve. However, they couldn't get the diabetic formula just right, and the tube scratched his esophagus. By Monday, he was in septic shock and died the next day. My siblings and I watched him take his last breath. At that point, because of his experience, I wished we'd taken him to hospice or home for a more peaceful experience. Though I have regrets, my peace is in knowing he has no more pain, and he's experiencing Heaven first hand.

Before Ed died, he told me, "I've had a rich life with great friends."

That was evident by the hundreds of people and friends who attended his celebration of life service and reception. He never married, didn't have much wealth, but was greatly loved by many who spoke of good times with him. Though Ed didn't have much of an estate, he left everything he had to my sister, whose life he saved. Without his small bit, she would have been homeless, so I applaud my brother who paid his blessings forward. Even after his short life, he provided. I hope he's celebrating up in Heaven!

Grief & Gratitude

"A person finds joy in giving an apt reply-and how good is a timely word!" (Proverbs 15:23)

Prayer: Heavenly Father, I am grateful that You always put your hand on me and guide my words. Thank You for your word which is the greatest love story ever told, and thank You for the opportunities to share the good news with others.

Deborah

"What can I do for you, Dad?" I asked.

"Could you wash my hair for me?" he replied.

My husband and I managed to move him, washed his hair and massaged his neck, which brought me full circle. You see, when I was a child I used to brush my dad's hair. My mother even showed me a picture a few years back of him reading his newspaper while I brushed his hair. So, during our Christmas holiday, with a diagnosis of stomach cancer and six months to live, I wanted to give him something that would serve him. Sadly, he died the next month on January 26th. This past year's Christmas was a fresh reminder of him.

With two brothers, I was Daddy's girl. I do believe there's a special bond between fathers and daughters that's like no other. Like our heavenly Father, my dad was a good provider, making sure our needs were met. He worked hard and I adored him. During my childhood, Dad wasn't a Christian but he surrendered himself to the Lord shortly before he passed, which gave me great solace. Coupled with that decision was my joy in doing something special and personal for him before his last dying breath.

You see, like Jesus himself, I want to give until my last breath. I'm someone who's faced numerous health issues but am grateful for breath each day, literally. Struggling with asthma, I appreciate just going for a walk in the warm sunshine. I know that God cares about every detail of my life and our lives, just like the slow, meticulous work of hair brushing. Though I don't know God's whole plan, or how many days he'll give me, I like to "run into the roar," taking a leap of faith no matter what I face.

For the past few years, I've ministered to others by writing poetry and praying for people who ask through social media. Like helping my father, that gives me purpose. I know no matter what tomorrow brings, I will trust God to direct my path, and have a joyful attitude until my last dying breath.

Grief & Gratitude

"Trust in the Lord with all your heart and lean not on your own understanding; in all your ways submit to him, and he will make your paths straight". (Proverbs 3:5,6)

Prayer: Heavenly Father, I am learning to trust You in all things and I am grateful that I don't have to direct my own life. Thank You for leading me on the right path.

Mark

"Why don't you come back for a visit?"

"No, I don't think so. Not yet," I replied.

I felt like an orphan. I couldn't go back to Kansas because I no longer had a "home" to go back to. It wasn't until 2009, when I was invited to my 30th high school reunion, that I made the trip back to my home town of Leavenworth. When I arrived, memories of my childhood flooded my mind. Most of those memories were pleasant and most were about Mom.

My father died in a car accident when I was two and my mother raised us alone. Mom diligently took care of me, made me a snack after school, and gave me advice or a hug when I needed it. After high school, I joined the military, serving in Germany from 1986 to 1995. I'd had a child and didn't want to leave, so I stayed and worked for the government until 2001.

While I was working overseas, Mom was struck with breast cancer, which spread to her brain. I was devastated. In a matter of months, she was gone.

At first, I felt angry. People would say, "Oh, I'm so sorry." Well, *sorry* is just a word people say when they don't know what else to say. I didn't want to hear *sorry* anymore! Those words were void. My thoughts were more like, "Why did she have to go through this? Why can't the medical field do more for cancer? Why doesn't the government allow for more cancer funding?"

Next, I felt depressed. I couldn't pick up the phone, like before, and call Mom when I wanted to talk. My daughter, who was named for my mom, never had a chance to form a relationship with her grandmother. Though I had siblings, I still felt alone after Mom passed. My brother and sisters each dealt with the loss in their own way. People who haven't lost a parent don't understand what that's like. When I observe people disrespecting their mom or dad, I get upset and tell them to love them because we don't know how long they'll be around. As a believer, I know the Bible says we're supposed to honor our parents.

Grief has different manifestations for different people but one thing I learned is I can't run from it, so I might as well face grief head on and embrace it. Personally, I experienced a mourning phase like no other but even on my darkest days, I didn't shut down. As time passed, I realized my ways are not God's ways. The good news, I believe, is that one day in Heaven, we'll rejoice and no longer mourn. Scripture promises us that, which gives me hope.

Grief & Gratitude

"Very truly I tell you, you will weep and mourn while the world rejoices. You will grieve, but your grief will turn to joy." (John 16:20)

Prayer: Holy God, I hurt so much when someone I love dies. When I face grief, I thank You that in time You take my ache away and bring me to a place of acceptance. Thank You that one day you will wipe all my tears away.

Renee

"Seen. Sought. I'm seen and I'm sought."

Those two words resonated with me, as I pondered them and asked the Lord about their significance. I believe they may be related to my past and the loss of my father.

At age 12, my dad suffered from clinical depression and took his own life. I remember the shock of being told he'd shot himself after my mother found him. Prior to that, I had a happy childhood, with two siblings, two parents and both sets of grandparents. Once he was gone, I felt alone. Different. Less than. I wanted to run away. Thankfully, my mom imparted to us that we weren't to be embarrassed and not to be ashamed of his suicide. We'd stay in our home. We'd be steadfast in our life.

As I grew into adolescence, I was very performance-driven and sought the attention of young men. Though I was fairly guarded as a teen and into college, I wanted the attention of a boyfriend. Yet I knew how to emotionally guard myself. I delved into alcohol and some drugs, which lessened my inhibitions and gave me a false sense of confidence. While I was hiding my true self, deep down I wanted someone to see me, to seek me, and pursue me. At the end of my sophomore year of college, a guy that I adored broke up with me and I had a panic attack. I was filled with anxiety and even had two days of observation in a hospital. During that dark time for me, I wondered whether I would end up like my dad. I remember being afraid of this spiritual battle, even though at the time I didn't know what spiritual warfare was.

On Sunday of that week, my aunt invited me to a church service, during which was an invitation. Though I didn't walk down to the altar, I prayed and felt the Holy Spirit come upon me. From that moment on, I trusted God with my life and I began to pray, read the Bible, and listen to anything I could that was Christian. I wanted to go deeper. I wanted to be seen and heard by God.

After college, I married and had two children. I'd desired a sweet caring man like my father but I had trouble fully trusting anyone. My dad, though he was depressed, was very likeable and I never doubted his love for me. However, after he died I found difficulty in trusting men. My husband is a bit like my father and has a great relationship with our daughter and that makes me happy as I see a picture of what "should have been," had my dad lived longer. More importantly, my husband is the ONE man who has ever pursued me - "seen" and "sought after" me. Yet over time God has revealed that He does the same for me.

Gratefully, I'm now an advocate for mental illness and suicide prevention. I'm a virtual volunteer for crisis intervention, which allows me to log onto my computer while teens and young adults text their issues. Though I never literally see them, I pray for God's protection over them and wisdom for myself as I log on and respond to them. It's as if I am speaking to them. I also love to talk in person to young people who don't have a great relationship with their parents, and it's my passion to pour into them, as a "spiritual mama." Just like me, they want to be seen and to be sought after. They are. And so am I.

Grief & Gratitude

"You will seek me and find me when you seek me with all your heart." (Jeremiah 29:13)

Prayer: Oh Lord, I am a seeker. I want to know You more and go deeper in my walk with You. I thank You that You saw me and pursued me, and love me unconditionally. I pray I may seek to be more like You every day of my life.

Cory

"Do you by chance have a photo of your husband, ma'am?"

When I answered the doorbell, two police officers stood there, sullen. They said there'd been a fatal car accident. Six months pregnant, I went numb and felt like I was having an out of body experience. Earlier that day I thought, oddly, that no one had heard from my husband Cameron. He left the house in the wee hours to play golf, while I left to go to work.

When I returned home that day, I was alarmed that Cameron's son from an earlier marriage had left several messages on the home. He asked why he hadn't picked him up for a medical appointment. In addition, his best friend called and asked me if I knew where he was because he couldn't reach him all day. Instinctively, I knew something was wrong but having called the local police and hospital with no answers, I was puzzled.

I must have been in shock because I asked the officers what I should do. They instructed me to go the hospital with his best friend, identify his body, and begin the process of alerting the rest of the family.

After the hospital staff prepared Cameron, his best friend and I had to identify his body. I made three calls: one to his ex-wife, one to my mother and one to my brother. I was foggy and unprepared, but knew I had to plan. Truthfully, for the next few days I was just going through the motions. People called and tried to console me, but I didn't feel anything. I ate for the sole reason I had a baby inside of me to feed. My mind was filled with lists of things I needed to do such as set up a nursery, purchase baby equipment, find daycare and find new people to support me, while working full time. I had to figure out LIFE as I now knew it.

One day at a time, I did figure out life. I didn't like that I had to do it by myself but I believed that God must have had a different plan for my life. What is interesting is that prior to my husband's passing, I was making the bed one day by myself and a random thought popped into my head: I would be a single mom and would raise my child on my own.

After his death, I was never angry but felt a bit "ripped off" that I didn't get to spend years with this man, and that my daughter would never know her dad. At first, I did ask the question, "Why?" This was definitely not the outcome I expected. I enjoyed the company of men, wanted to get married, and have children like most women. Thankfully, I did have the support of a "village" – family, friends, and babysitters who helped so I could work and live my life.

Everyone deals with grief differently. You shouldn't listen to what people "think" is best for you. If you need to read a book, read it! If you need to get counseling, get it! If you want to date or remarry, do it! For me, taking one day at a time, one thing at a time, one relationship at a time was best. Now, 21 years later, I am blessed with a new marriage and thankful that is part of the "plan."

Grief & Gratitude

"For my thoughts are not your thoughts, neither are your ways my ways," declares the Lord. (Isaiah 55:8)

Prayer: God, I'm grateful that although things didn't turn out how I expected them to, You had a bigger plan. Despite my grief, thank You for the many blessings on the journey.

V icki

"Are you afraid of death?" I asked him.

"A little," he responded.

"Are you afraid of where you are going, or just afraid of the process?

"The process."

My husband of 33 years was lying in his hospital bed and we were coming to grips with his rare illness and disappointing prognosis. After two years of trials and medications, nothing was working to cure this form of intestinal cancer. I never stopped praying for a miracle, up until Steve's last breath.

I don't even use the word *death* to this day. I prefer the term *passed.* Though it's been ten years, not a day goes by that I don't miss Steve and all that we shared. We had a great life, with two sons, and we were both enjoying retirement. We were soul mates.

Steve was very humble, and the most selfless person I ever knew. He was a health nut, ate well, and exercised so we were surprised when we received the news of his cancer diagnosis. Shocked? You bet. Angry? Not so much, but I felt disappointed.

I love God and am a woman of faith, but nothing prepares you for those words. The doctor had warned me when he went into surgery that we might face cancer, but I still held out hope. When we found out, I fell to pieces, but we did all we could to fight this tumor which had ruptured his intestine. I could not imagine my life without my loving husband and soul mate.

I was halfway through my training as a Stephens minister at church when Steve fell ill. As part of my training, I assisted others in the loss of their husbands or children, but this was different. Nothing is like the loss of your own spouse.

When Steve passed that September, I remember just staring out into space, not sure of what to do. I was empty. I learned what true wailing

74

is like. When friends invited me over for New Year's Eve, which was our tradition for years, I couldn't go. Instead, I stayed home and watched movies and cried. My worst hours were from 11 pm-2am, and sometimes I would ask a friend to come over just to "babysit" me. Thankfully, a widow told me, "You have permission to cry. You have permission to do whatever you want. Don't listen to what awkward people tell you to do. Do what is good for you."

After the new year, I took a trip with my son to Orlando, and trips with both sons for each year after that. Those trips felt right. I celebrated my birthday because Steve made a big deal of it, and would have wanted me to. I saw other couples holding hands and wasn't sad, but happy for them and grateful for the years we'd had. I continued with the philanthropy that he and I started, and I completed my Stephen's ministry training, becoming a caregiver to other widows. Most importantly, I began to write again. However, my writing was now different.

Prior to retirement, I wrote technical pieces such as business letters and a customer care guide for work. I never wrote warm and fuzzy things. In fact, when someone would send an email like that, instead of crying, I couldn't delete the note fast enough! After Steve passed, however, I found I wanted to write about softer things. I wanted to introduce people to the person my husband was. I began to write and write, and before I knew it, I had 10 short stories published. Truly, writing became a catharsis for my pain.

I've learned a few things about death:

First, some people view death as punishment. However, as a Christian, I read what the Bible tells me: death is not punishment and Heaven is our reward. How could there be anything better? While we hope for our loved ones to live, and perhaps for a different diagnosis, we can have an assurance of their peace and eternal life with God, if they've received Him.

Second, I don't worry about death and I don't fear it. I live alone, and I have often thought that if I were to die alone, I wouldn't technically be alone. I know where I am going, and I know that I will be reunited with my loved ones, not to mention the wonderful peace of Heaven. In fact, I've come close to dying with different health scares, but I no longer fear it.

Lastly, I've learned to count my blessings. I am so grateful to have had those talks with Steve prior to his passing and to plan his memorial service. I was blessed by his love for 33 years. Though sometimes you can get hung up on regrets of what you "should have" done, I have learned that God is still in charge no matter what, that He knew the days of Steve's life, and that I had to face the grief. I also couldn't see things like juggling two houses and trying to sell one while the housing market fell as a blessing, but in hindsight, I can now see that gave me time to go through my things, slowly, and to let go of some things.

Grief takes time to work through, and grief means you must face the pain head on. Remember, you have permission to cry. You have permission to do what you need to do to heal. For me, that is writing and ministering to others.

Grief & Gratitude

"And let us consider how we may spur one another on toward love and good deeds." (Hebrews 10:24)

Prayer: Gracious God, thank You for your comfort when we are weak and no one else can comfort us. Thank You for your healing, whether it comes immediately, over time, or when we are with You in Heaven.

R_{ita}

"They're coming for me. You'll see."

"Mike, what are you talking about? Who is coming after you?"

"You know what's going on," he replied.

The fact is, I didn't know what was going on. I was confused. Here was my husband of 40 years, who I'd known and loved since we were teenagers, and I was frightened. As a therapist, I know that you can admit someone to a hospital for 24 hours. After that, they can choose to stay or check out. Mike was checking out.

Back when we first courted, Mike was adopted by my parents and loved being part of such a family. His own home life wasn't great; with eight siblings, he was seen as the "hero," since he was self-reliant and self-sufficient. He was my hero as well, and we were soul mates.

After college, Mike's dream was to be a dentist so we lived in a less than desirable neighborhood in Richmond, Virginia, while he completed his dental school. We had a new baby and were broke, and I was lonely. Eventually, we moved back up north to be near my family and he started his own dental practice. Raised Catholics, we were invited to a neighborhood Bible study and began to dig into the Bible and our personal walk with Christ. We both took our faith to a deeper level and Mike even sometimes preached at local events. We were active in a grass roots pro-life ministry, rescuing babies and women who were seeking abortions. Not much time passed before Mike was president of the board of directors and later helped build an orphanage in Nicaragua. At one point, he even wondered if he should be a pastor instead of a dentist. However, he chose the dental practice and gave hundreds of hours and dollars of free dental care to needy patients. The office itself was a ministry.

When my father became ill, he moved in with us, and I worked on my bachelor's and master's degrees in counseling. I went to work at a local counseling practice, and Mike was supportive, but he slowly dropped out of his own commitments. He took up flying lessons, got his pilot's license, and bought a plane. However, he had some serious internal struggles and demons he needed to work out. In 2012, when his sister was in the hospital and came close to dying, Mike realized he was angry at God for some things, which was a pivotal moment. He claimed Psalm 73. He bounced back temporarily, but I noticed after a while he became very emotional and paranoid.

Mike believed he was being "watched" and he was the target of some conspiracy. Much was due to circumstantial events like his malpractice insurance and his pilot insurance policies being cancelled. I learned later that these were simple changes the companies made, nothing due to Mike's negligence or fault. To further his anxiety and paranoia, Mike read an article in a dental magazine about a dentist who was sued for a Medicare billing mistake, and went to prison for two years. One night he said to me, "I can't live if I go to prison."

I encouraged Mike at this point to go see a psychiatrist, and to take medication for his anxiety. While he did take a mild anti-depressant, he refused other medications, and in a fit of fear, came home one night and threw out an entire cabinet of all our pills. Mike also kept a gun collection.

One day I came home and couldn't find him in the house. I heard a gunshot and screamed, running through the house looking for him. I ran outside in a field behind our home and saw him coming down the hill with a gun in hand. I thought he'd tried to kill himself. I called a pastor to come talk with him, and Mike didn't even acknowledge that he had an issue. I took him to a local psychiatric hospital and after staying the afternoon, he checked himself out. He felt that no one could help him.

During this time, my counseling practice had expanded and I'd published a book. I was on the road promoting it, doing a radio show, and Mike joined me briefly, in Florida. We owned a second home on the coast and planned for retirement there. Prior to going, Mike agreed to spend some time at the Meier clinic in Dallas, for evaluation, knowing he was severely depressed. We agreed that after flying back to Virginia, he would take a break from his work at the dental office and go to Dallas. I had a commitment that Monday, so he flew home without me, and had dinner with our son and daughter-in-law. I tried calling him that night, but got no answer. I did confirm with my son that he came, and he reported that they had some concerns about him but let him go home.

On Tuesday morning, before I flew home, I called Mike again from the airport, and got no answer. I began to panic. I knew that he was supposed to pick up some blood work results from his doctor's office, so I called them and they confirmed that he had done that in the morning. I felt more at ease. When I landed, I tried him again and got no answer. Panic again. Pulling up to our house in the taxi, I saw his car and the garage open and was confused. Why wasn't he at work? Why was the garage open?

When I walked in, I found his gym bag and his Bible on the floor. I walked up the stairs, down the hallway and saw him. Mike was lying in our bedroom, covered in blood and dead from a gunshot. I let out a primal scream. I touched him and ran down the stairs. Crouched in a corner, I called my son and he screamed. I called my sister in law who told me to stay on the phone, and someone else called an ambulance.

All I remember next is that the police came, asked some questions, and the rest was a fog. The whole episode was surreal. My son and daughter were in as much shock as I was. We all felt regrets and wondered what we could have done differently. With one delusional act, he was gone. Where was he? I was despondent myself. Widowed at 59, I had lost my soul mate.

After Mike's memorial service, I still could not function. As time passed, I insisted on having someone at the house by my side. I did not want to live. In the dark soul of the night, I wailed and felt nothing other than the presence of God. As a devout follower of Christ, I knew that Mike was in the arms of God, no longer suffering. However, my pain didn't disappear.

Mike had a huge estate to take care of which caused major stress for so long. Because of the trauma of finding him, I fought nightmares and still do to this day. I had two major episodes of PTSD, but with the help of counselors and friends, I survived them. God showed up in miraculous ways. Through EMDR therapy, visions, and powerful imagery, God has given me a new breath of life. He has exchanged my ashes for beauty.

Within a year following my loss, I joined a suicide grief group and began doing some self-care again. With no intention of ever marrying again, I went out on a few dates with men because I missed the company of a man and I'm a relational person. On one date, I met a man who had a lot in common with me – a widower about the same age as me, with adult children and many of the same interests I had. Having faced his own loss, he helped me so much. After dating for months, one day he proposed. We've been married over a year and he is a huge blessing to me.

Though I never thought I could marry again, I realize that Mike is now in a "glorified state" in Heaven, and when we meet again, our relationship will not be as marriage partners. Some days are more difficult than others, but I'm learning to live one day at a time without my soul mate.

Grief & Gratitude

"Have mercy on me, my God, have mercy on me, for in you I take refuge. I will take refuge in the shadow of your wings until the disaster has passed." (Psalm 57:1)

Prayer: Abba Father, I'm so sad and lost at times. The only thing I am assured of is your presence and I am grateful for that. You are a good God and I thank You for comforting and carrying me through the darkest soul of the night.

Barbara

"What happened? Where am I?"

I was confused. My mother and sister were hovering over me, glad I was awake after a two- week coma.

"You were in a bad car accident, hit by a drunk driver on December 18th."

My mind immediately focused on Curtis, my husband of 18 years, and I assumed he was lying in a hospital bed near me, perhaps recovering from injuries. When I asked, they hesitated before saying, "Curtis is in Heaven, and the driver died as well."

Those words gripped me like a wrench. I felt darkness and despair. I didn't want to continue living without Curtis. I had no hope and no desire to go on. I felt very alone and cried out to the Lord. Since I was still in ICU and had several broken bones and surgeries to face, I watched TV when I could. One day, I heard a pastor who talked about God's grace and mercy even in our circumstances. That helped me see a small glimmer of hope. When I told my sister I had no blessings left, she reminded me that I could see, hear, and speak. That the sun was shining through my hospital room window. That one day I would walk again. She was right!

Though the doctors told me that I'd need up to a year and a half to walk again, I'm grateful I walked within four months. Because I had two broken legs, two broken arms, a damaged pelvis and more, I had a long road to recovery. I spent many hours in therapy and struggled along the way. Some days I missed my husband so much, but then I remembered the bass guitar he wanted and we couldn't afford. I was convinced that he got one in Heaven and that he was part of the praise team there, which brought me joy.

When we first met, Curtis had been praying for a wife. Unbeknownst to me at the time, when he sat across from me at a church meeting, he told his friend, "That's the girl I'm going to marry." His friend reminded him that he didn't even know my name, but he didn't care. We married that year and had some great years together, working odd jobs together and serving in ministry together. When I was in the hospital and felt depressed, I would remember those things and start to thank God for the many blessings we had.

After my long rehabilitation, I gave my testimony on TV, on a radio show, and in a small book I wrote. I have been able to minister to many people who have struggled with their health or tragedy or are widowed. Likewise, I am so grateful to the many people who prayed for me after the accident and during my healing process. Many people sent me emails when I was in ICU, and the medical staff would deliver them to me. Those kept me going some days!

At first, I couldn't forgive the drunk driver who took my husband's life. After several years, I reached out to the man's mother on Thanksgiving and sent her a note. I let her know that I was sure she was struggling with her loss, just as I was, but that I held no resentment in my heart for her son, and that I hoped he was in Heaven along with my Curtis. I never heard back from her but I am free knowing that I have forgiven. Gratefully, I'm able to walk again and most of all my joy is restored. Before I step out of bed each morning, I thank God for that.

Grief & Gratitude

"Restore to me the joy of your salvation and grant me a willing spirit, to sustain me". (Psalm 51:12)

Prayer: Gracious Father, I am so grateful that You have restored me. Though I should be dead, You have given me hope and a purpose for my life. Please grant me a willing spirit to do your work and share with others what You have done for me.

Teresa

I was working on my profile for an online dating site when I thought, "I am NOT going to compromise myself, even if this is not a Christian site. I'm still adamant that I'm only going to date a man with the same commitment."

I'd made the commitment to myself and to God that I didn't need a man to make me complete. My heart's desire was to marry again, but I was content if God's will was for me to be single. Once I did that, I felt free. I met Gary, my third husband, after that. He responded to my post and we began to talk through email, for three or four weeks, before we met face to face. Of course, I had my trust issues to work through.

I married my high school sweetheart at 19 and after 32 years together, he told me he was not happy and wanted a divorce. I learned that he was having an affair with another woman and this hurt me more than anything. After being together so long, that made no sense to me. I still believed that he would come home and I prayed that he still loved me. Sadly, he did not, which was the beginning of a long, hard journey. For the first few weeks, I leaned on my family and friends for support. I played music all day, read books, and clung to God. During that first year, I grew closer to God than ever before, and felt the Holy Spirit come over me. I felt His healing, although not overnight.

I experienced the typical stages of grief, including depression. I remember that because I had no appetite, I did not eat and made myself ill. At one point, I lost 70 pounds in 10 months and I ended up in the emergency room. The depression was so overwhelming that I could not see the light at the end of the tunnel. I moved into my daughter's home and the darkness continued to weigh me down. Eight years after my divorce, anger hit me all at once. I sought out a counselor, who allowed me to have my pity party for a maximum of five minutes!

In my loneliness and desperation for love, and being smitten with the idea of being in love, I met someone and married again. I saw the red flags and warning signals in advance, but I married him anyway. When he left me after 18 months, I was not devastated. I just told God I didn't care if I ever married or ever loved again. He'd have to show me if marrying again was His will or not. That's when I let go.

At that point, God was teaching me that He loved me, He knew what tomorrow would bring, and that He had my back. I never felt complete without a man, and now I did. I knew that God was enough. I had a heart for women who were hurting and even started a singles ministry at church. I felt complete.

Because of God's mercy and grace, I eventually met Gary. We've been married for one year and I'm grateful to God that He showed me I could trust Him and that he honored my desires. At one time, nothing made sense to me. Now, by trusting in Him and His path, and not my own, everything made sense.

As the saying goes, "Three times is a charm!"

Grief & Gratitude

"Take delight in the Lord, and he will give you the desires of your heart." (Psalm 37:4)

Prayer: Precious Lord, I spent so many years searching for someone to love. I thank You for answering my prayers in a way that only You could. Most of all, thank You for delighting me.

G_{reg}

"My wife is lying on the floor hysterical…I have done some horrible things in our marriage…we need some help, please!" I was desperate.

The gentleman explained that he was just the church accountant and that the pastor was gone, and could call back after Christmas. I told him most likely, I wouldn't have a marriage after Christmas. You see, I had been down this road before with two previous marriages, and was desperate to save this one plus concerned about what might happen to my unborn child.

I am a preacher's son. I know all about the Bible and adultery and yet I still managed to jump from woman to woman. After graduating from college, I married a wonderful Christian woman and we had a son. After being married for several years, I attended a high school reunion and hooked up with an old friend, caught up in a seductive fantasy. That relationship broke up her marriage and mine. When I told my first wife I was leaving, she wrapped her arms around my leg and begged me to stay. Like a fool, I turned my back on her, literally, and walked out. I remember pointing my finger at God and saying, "You've let me down." As if I deserved more.

From there, I went from being a gentle guy to a reprobate. I lived an extremely dark lifestyle of moral decadence. I had finished law school, was a successful partner in a law firm, but could not stop my wandering eye. Sadly, I carried that into the second marriage. I am not sure to this day how many women I hurt or how many children I may have fathered. However, I know there were more than a few and part of the reason for my brokenness. I finally entered counseling.

After years of seeking counsel and taking stock of my life, I met my third wife. She was quite a bit younger than me and was aware of my adulterous past, but was willing to marry me and work through my issues with me. As the years passed and we had two children, her trust in me waned. At her request, I gave her access to my phone and emails but she still felt she couldn't trust me. When she felt enraged, she even threw objects at me. So, two days before Christmas we made a desperate cry for help.

When the pastor of the small church called back, he suggested that one of his parishioners who had done some counseling come over and meet us. We agreed. During our meeting, he told me he wasn't sure if I was in fact sorry for all the things I'd done to her and to other women, or I was just "sorry" indeed. He instructed me to compose an email to all the women I'd been with, explaining my remorse and to cut off further contact with all of them. He instructed me to send a letter of resignation to my law partners, and to go to a Sexual Addicts group meeting for six months. I did all three.

During this time, my wife found out that I'd once been unfaithful to her with my former wife. She felt injured, could not forgive me, and filed for divorce a little over a year ago.

Though infidelity and divorce are extremely painful, one good thing that came of my brokenness and the consequences that followed is I got involved with a ministry called Tres Dias. It's a ministry that helps families in crisis. I also have an accountability group of men for my addiction. Currently, I speak to others about my experience, and how I was led by an enemy who comes to steal, kill, and destroy marriages.

I have not lost my hope and belief that God uses all things – and even allows them at times - for His glory. Though I grieve for my children and their perspective on this, I am confident that God is not interested in my happiness. He is interested in my **righteousness.**

Grief & Gratitude

"In you, Lord, I have taken refuge; let me never be put to shame; deliver me in your righteousness." (Psalm 31:1)

Prayer: Abba Father, I have made many mistakes for which I am sorry. I am grateful that You are merciful and forgive me. Make me righteous in your sight, oh God.

P am

"I am done with you. We're over. I've found someone else."

Those words don't sting quite as much as they did back then, but I still remember that pivotal point when I realized my life would be forever changed. My husband of 35 years had met another woman and decided to leave the marriage and everything we'd built. In truth, we were struggling before then, as I'd been ill and had multiple surgeries prior to the affair. So much for "in sickness and in health."

I thought when I married at 19, that this was once and for all, and I would spend the rest of my life with my husband. In fact, I was never one to have the goal of getting married at the top of my list, but I was young, trusted him as a friend first, and eventually fell in love.

Over the next few years, we had more struggles than I could have imagined. We moved seven times, so he could build his career and we found our way to Florida. I started my own career over several times so I could be supportive, and I put my Christian faith and church on hold due to our differences. Finally, I knew that God was calling me back to Himself, and even my husband couldn't keep me from that. I was going deeper with God and he didn't like it, even calling me a "Bible thumper" at times. Thinking back, I'd made an idol out of my husband, and served him for so many years before God made clear to me that He must come first. Though I hoped and prayed for reconciliation after finding out about the affair, I never let go of what I had to do. I went to counseling. I went to Divorce Care. I even had pity parties, but realized you had to put a start and stop time on those. I put one foot in front of the other. Some days I didn't want to talk to anyone, including God.

After three years of senseless and expensive legal battles, my husband finally agreed to the terms of the divorce. Prior to that, he lied in court, we exchanged words, and we spent thousands of dollars in legal fees. I told him, "You have to stop this!" Mind you, I don't believe in divorce and I tell others the same, but I had due reason, and I'm not accountable for the actions of my ex-husband.

I'm more at peace now and see God's hand in every area of my life. When finances were impossible, He made a way. I have a darling townhouse with a dream mortgage, two dogs, a new car, and a job with retirement benefits. At one time, during the separation, I thought I might wind up homeless. In fact, I asked God to humble me no matter what the circumstances were, and yet He was merciful. I now have the privilege of serving in a homeless ministry, listening to others' stories and praying with them. I know how blessed I am.

As I reflect on my marriage and my divorce, I admit trust doesn't come naturally and I'm working on that. I don't date, for the time being, and I am content. I have a good life and I trust that if God has marriage for me in the future, He will bring that to pass. Although I worry at times, and I've had some health scares, I know that God is protecting me and is leading me.

Everyone has a different experience. I tell other women not to go through divorce blindly. Get counseling if needed. Go to support groups. Don't listen to everyone's unsolicited advice but listen to God and follow Him. No doubt He will lead you down the right path.

Grief & Gratitude

"When anxiety was great within me, your consolation brought me joy." (Psalm 94:19)

Prayer: Dear God, how I thank You for removing my anxious heart and replacing it with a new, joyful one. Though I never wanted a divorce, I trust that You pardoned me from a tarnished marriage and I am forever grateful for your protection and provision.

Deana

"I didn't even know you were pregnant!"

"Well, we were all a bit surprised," I nervously chuckled as I held baby Cameron.

That was one of a few defining moments.

Months earlier, I opened my email to find a picture of a baby with an explanation that my husband had fathered him. I stared at the computer screen in shock. We had just started to heal our relationship, and he'd moved back in with the girls and me after his skin cancer diagnosis. About a year before that, after an 18-year marriage, I found out that he'd had an affair with a 25-year-old. After the initial shock, we decided to face our crisis head-on.

We had two daughters, 12 and 16 at the time, and we wanted to be honest with them without sugar coating anything. He moved out and we began to make the best of our new separation, with me being a single parent most of the time.

When the phone call about his cancer came and he asked me if I would help him get through it, I agreed. He came back home to live with us while he had his surgery and treatments. Easier said than done. Our marriage was strained and I would sometimes leave the house to go to my mother's so I could let the flood of tears come without my girls seeing it. Even my mom didn't know the depths of my pain.

Faced with a baby who wasn't ours, I wondered how we would cope. How could we explain this to our girls? Or to our friends in the community? I do believe that God is aware of everything, and that He allows things to happen for a purpose, but I needed to know how my husband wanted to proceed. Did he want to be part of the baby's life even if he wasn't involved with the mother anymore? He said he wanted to be involved and because I wanted to take the higher road and be a loving example to our girls, I agreed. We shared custody with the mother of this young child for two years. However, inside I was broken.

During this time, I had a lot of time to reflect on our marriage. I had time to breathe and ask myself questions like: What do I want in 20 years? What does my husband want? When the kids are gone, will our relationship be different? Another defining moment. I decided to talk with him and let him know I had some needs that were not being met.

Mind you, we had every possible material thing – a 5500 square foot home on three acres, a boat, jet skis, truck of the year, yet none of those things mattered to me. I spoke to him and saw some changes; however, they were short-lived. He went back to his old ways. He also went back to his girlfriend.

At this point, I moved into a small apartment and decided to do some soul-searching. I joined new sports groups, met new friends, and learned how to be happy with just being by myself. I continued to pray, to go to church and to question if my marriage would ever change. I did the one thing I knew how to do: I released everything over to God.

I checked out some online dating sites and even had coffee with a few guys. I had made my "list" and I had high standards which I never thought could be met. One day, I met a man who was a great father and had a sense of adventure. I was still shy about commitment and still did not trust men. However, he patiently pursued me.

When I was out of state visiting a friend, we were driving from the airport and witnessed a head-on fatal car accident. Another defining moment. I knew at that moment that God was giving me a sign, saying "It's okay. Life is very short and fragile. This man loves you and has everything on your list, so don't be foolish. Marry him."

Five years have passed and I am so blessed now. I understand that a child born out of wedlock and adultery could be a blessing, just as my new husband is. God's plan painted a much bigger and better picture than I could have ever imagined, and my pain was to His glory.

Grief & Gratitude

"Consider it pure joy, my brothers and sisters, whenever you face trials of many kinds, because you know that the testing of your faith produces perseverance." (James 1:2-3)

Prayer: Dear Lord, I don't like facing big trials in my life, but I am grateful that You bring me through them. Thank You so much for your mercy and grace, as You mature me in the process.

J ackie

"I'm not happy. I hate this house. I hate this yard and I hate this dog!"

"Nobody can hate an old Lab. What are you talking about?"

"I want a divorce." His words stunned me.

"I'm sorry. I'm sorry!" I sobbed.

I remember grabbing hold of our kitchen cabinet, clinging to anything I could, and not believing what I was hearing. That was a memory crystallized in my mind. That moment was a defining moment for us. I could kick myself now for saying those words. I wasn't the one who should have been apologizing. Brad was the one who'd betrayed me. At the time, all I could think of were our two boys and what this would do to them.

When I first met him, I was smitten. Brad was a new teacher in our school and unlike anyone I'd ever met. He was charismatic, a bit rogue and wild. I hadn't dated since my sweet beau in college, and I was hesitant about caring for anyone else after he died. While we were dating in the summer before my junior year, he was tragically killed as a consequence of a misfired gunshot. His death rocked my world and I wasn't sure I could love again.

When Brad pursued me, I introduced him to my parents who loved him. He formed a special relationship with my father. Daddy was my hero and we shared a wonderful bond since I was his only daughter. He owned a produce plant, was a very successful business man and a caring community steward. Involved in our church, he never missed an opportunity to teach me valuable lessons.

I remember the time I woke up in a bad mood. I just wanted to stay there, but Daddy wouldn't let me. He insisted we go down and see Amos, the man who was missing two legs and never in a "bad mood." I fought him, but after seeing Amos, I learned that lesson quickly.

After a year or two of teaching, Brad decided he didn't like that career and my dad asked him to join his company. They were a great team – a combination of Daddy's great personality and customer care along with Brad's good work ethic. When we married, they were instant friends and good partners. Later, we had two sons, 22 months apart, while I was still working full-time and going to school for my master's degree. Between family and all of our friends, we had no shortage of babysitters in our small town of Andalusia, Alabama. Life was good.

In 1977, Daddy suffered his first heart attack. In those days, no bypass surgeries were done, so he was told to go home and take a daily baby aspirin. At 56, he was slender and active so he slowed down a bit. A year later, he had a more serious heart attack but still didn't quit working. By 1980, he had his third and final heart attack, which knocked all of us down. We were all lost, not knowing what we were going to do without him. Everyone needs a cheerleader in their life and Daddy was mine. He was so proud of me for being a teacher and I could do no wrong in his eyes.

After Daddy's death, life in my small town began to change and I admit that I was a bit oblivious to it. We lived in my grandparent's old farmhouse and devoted ourselves to refurbishing it, which gave me something on which to focus. Brad continued to run the business and brought in a new partner to help him, while I taught middle school English. I continued to raise our boys, going to all their sporting events. Perhaps I doted on them too much but isn't that what moms are supposed to do?

Brad began to slack off in managing the business and sold it. He went back to teaching in a small town next to the one where I taught. Life was good, so I thought.

One day, he came home and said he needed to talk. I just thought he was in a bad mood, until he proceeded to tell me all the things that he hated.

"So, you hate me too," I cried.

"No, I don't hate you, I'm just not happy."

"Well, we can move. I will go anywhere you want to. Please just don't do this!"

"No, I won't take this house from you. That house belongs in your family. I will move out."

I still begged Brad not to do this to our sons and to me. I asked him to join me for marriage counseling which he refused, saying we were smarter than any counselor. I couldn't imagine what divorce would do to my boys. They were all I could think about at that moment. In truth, Brad said I showed more attention to them than to him, which hurt him. Little did I know at the time, he was getting plenty of attention. Unfortunately, that attention wasn't coming from me.

Not long after he moved out and into an apartment, a friend called me. I had plenty of friends and people in town who were empathetic to my situation and ready to give advice. This good friend asked me a pointed question one day which started my wheels spinning.

"Jackie, do you think he's got someone else on the side?"

"Well, no, I don't think so," I responded.

"If he did, would you want to know?" she asked.

"Yes, I would."

Next, she told me what I never wanted to hear: that he was seeing someone else. She was a fellow teacher and someone who'd been to my home before. To say I felt betrayed is an understatement. However, that did not prevent me from confronting him about her. Of course, he denied everything. I wanted to believe him, but things just didn't add up.

Through the advice of others, I contacted a lawyer to protect myself and my boys, which helped me lay some groundwork. Though my husband thought he was smart, his arrogance harmed him. After many months, we divorced.

One day I was sitting out on a lawn chair behind my farmhouse, anxious and unable to handle my losses anymore. Praying to God, I told Him I'd give everything-all my cares- to Him. I'd said that previously yet tried to handle things myself. That day I prayed and felt a burden removed. My heart felt lighter. I stopped crying. I heard His voice say, "You're going to be all right." That was a turning point for me.

My two sons became wonderful men despite the divorce. I continued to follow them to their sporting events throughout middle and high school, and settled into being a single mom. I didn't date anyone for many years because I had trouble trusting anyone and didn't want my boys investing in someone who might not be around for the long haul. Mind you, I had many invitations to dinner but I was just not interested. The word got out quick that I wasn't available! My heart was shut down because I needed to learn to trust again. Months later, I got a call from Jerry.

Jerry was someone I knew from college, but we were just friends. When he called, he shared his condolences about my predicament. He'd moved to St. Louis after college and returned to Alabama, single with no children. When he suggested we go for dinner and talk, I asked if he meant for a date. When he said yes, I declined. I was not ready. He would call from time to time, and one day he invited me to a football game. I love sports so I agreed to meet him there.

From that day on, we took our time and dated six years. When my youngest son was preparing to graduate from high school, Jerry told me he wanted to be with us permanently. I knew he was a wonderful guy and trustworthy, so I agreed. We married that year.

During my divorce and afterward, I went for counseling which I believe helped me. My therapist taught me some good techniques and I learned to let go. Since then, I've also been able to minister to some of my own friends who've faced their own betrayals. I share the Bible with them, and show them some verses which are applicable. I love the Psalms and Proverbs since they are both like poetry, and as a retired English teacher, I can appreciate that. One thing my dad told me, which I think rings true today, is:

A lot of dating is learning who you DON'T want to marry. Daddy sure was a wise man!

Grief & Gratitude

"Cast all your anxiety on him because he cares for you." (1 Peter 5:7)

Prayer: Dear Lord, I thank You that You are someone I can lean on for all my cares and concerns. You are my greatest cheerleader and I am grateful for your wisdom. I thank You for being my father when mine was gone, and for being a father to my sons when they needed one. I thank You for second chances at love and for delighting me with the desires of my heart.

Mary Beth

"There's something wrong with your baby," the doctor said.

The paper I was to sign said the procedure was called a medical abortion. Oh no, I wasn't going to do that. This was my baby. I prayed, "Lord, please show me what to do, that this is your plan."

Because I did not experience a miscarriage, and the baby no longer had a heartbeat and not able to live outside my womb, I had a medical D&C.

I went into shock immediately. I thought I was dreaming, but when I woke up I realized I wasn't and had difficulty coming to terms with the loss. My husband and I'd had one healthy baby girl and we wanted more children. We were both emotionally shut down though many people tried to encourage us. They said things like, "You'll have another baby. You'll be pregnant in no time ", or "That was God's will."

What some people don't understand is that one baby does not take the place of another one. The other misnomer is that God "takes" a baby from you as part of His will. Not true! That said, I believed that my baby was with God in Heaven. I hoped that he or she would be comforted and whole. One of the best things someone told me was that when you're in the pit, God crawls right in with you and stays with you until you are ready to come out. Satan will try to tell you lies and destroy you through self-blame, pointing a finger at God, or bringing marital dissension. Thankfully, I knew that God was a loving god who had me in the palm of His hand and knew what the future would bring. He also used our doctor to speak life back into my husband and me. He encouraged us to try for another baby which helped recreate some intimacy for us.

Two years later, I was pregnant again and had a "normal" pregnancy. However, I worried a lot about a second miscarriage and was afraid to be hopeful. I felt robbed of joy, in a sense, until our sweet second daughter, Sarah, was born. God showed me that she would be fine. We had a third child, a son, and felt our family was complete. After my oldest got married and had two daughters of her own, we experienced the joy of grandchildren, knowing ALL blessings are from God. He does not "take away" our loved ones, but allows things to happen, which prepared me for what was going to happen in the future.

My daughter Sarah married a wonderful military man and was a stepmom to his children, before trying to have their own. When she was five months pregnant, her husband was deployed to Afghanistan. She was on her way home from a visit with us when her water broke, and she was not able to get to the hospital before one of the twins' feet came through the birth canal. Usually, a medical team can stop the labor process with a shot but hers was not the case.

My husband and I jumped in our car and rushed to Arizona so that we could be with her. In the hospital there was a special ward where they deliver babies who are not born alive, which is where Sarah was. Unfortunately, her doctor did not have a good bedside manner and was stoic. Gratefully, her nurse was caring and helped her give birth to the babies, one at a time. Thankfully, they didn't suffer. In fact, the nurse cleaned the babies and dressed them in preemie clothes and my daughter named them and held them. We cried together, while imagining their personalities and that brought some closure for us as well as her husband, once he arrived.

This past year Sarah gave birth to a healthy baby girl and we all spent time loving on her. I realize that her baby will not ever replace the two she lost, just as mine did not replace the one I lost. And though her experience in the hospital and mine were completely different, I could minister to her, reminding her that the miscarriage was not her fault. I reminded her that God didn't "take" her babies away and that she was loved.

I think that's all we can do for someone who experiences loss and is grieving. We hold them. We love them. We can offer to do things for them like fold laundry or make meals. We remind them that God loves them and loves their lost loved one. He knows every hair on our heads, every cell in our bodies, and holds us in the palm of His hand.

Grief & Gratitude

"Your eyes saw my unformed body; all the days ordained for me were written in your book before one of them came to be." (Psalm 139:16)

Prayer: Father, thank You that You are the creator of life and know every hair on our heads and every cell in our bodies. I am so grateful that even when a life is gone, You redeem that loss with new life and new hope.

Hope

"What in the name of God have you done to this child?!"

The emergency room was full of people glaring at us, while I held my three-week old limp baby in my arms. I panicked and did not respond. I can't remember much about that day or leaving the hospital after she was gone. At that time, the military didn't tell you much and we didn't ask many questions. We were just grateful they didn't call the MP's on us.

October 28, 1960 was a beautiful fall day in Junction City, Kansas. The leaves of autumn were gorgeous as we noted from my hospital room. I had just given birth to our first baby girl, Susan, and life was good. She joined our toddler Dennis, and my husband and I were rejoicing. Unlike her brother, Susan didn't each much or gain much weight in those three weeks we were at home, but any time she cried, I was attentive and would warm up a bottle for her.

One Saturday afternoon, I was lying on the couch, watching TV in our small trailer home. Both children were taking a nap when I heard Susan cry. I got up, made her a bottle, but by the time I went back to her small bassinette, she was already asleep. I went back to the couch and fell asleep.

About an hour later, our boxer Duchess came and licked me on the face, and was pacing from the front room to the back of the trailer. I asked my husband, Denny, to go and see why he was doing that. Once he did, he called out to me, "Hope, something is wrong with the baby."

I jumped up and went back to check on her, and picked her up. She was limp as a dish rag. Her body was still warm but her face was colorless. We ran and got a neighbor to watch our son, while we jumped in the car.

On the way to the hospital, I attempted CPR on our baby girl. I was beside myself. I couldn't talk and Denny began to vomit once we were there. I tried my best to compose myself and answer questions of the staff. They told us that Susan was gone. I felt like a robot, going through the motions but not functioning. We left the hospital without our precious baby girl.

Early the next morning, about four o'clock, I do remember hanging wet diapers out on our clothesline. We called our parents, who came thereafter, as we were traumatized. My mother-in-law ranted that we had neglected our baby and blamed us for her death. We were terrified that our toddler son had forced a bottle into her mouth or hurt her. We were still in shock. My mother told me later that when she came for the memorial service, I was dressed up and stoic as I welcomed guests like we were hosting a tea party. I think I'd been prescribed phenobarbital and was reacting like a zombie.

Three weeks later, at my six-week postpartum checkup, the doctor asked me how my baby was doing. When I replied that she had passed away, he asked, "How?" The truth was I still didn't know. Thankfully, he cared enough to find out so we made our way down to the autopsy records department, where I was told that Susan died of "crib death," which we currently call Sudden Infant Death Syndrome. We were still curious about any possible secondary cause, like my prenatal smoking, but were assured that wasn't the case. Nonetheless, I was still unstable.

Soon after, Denny received orders for Korea, and left the following month. During this time, my son came down with pneumonia and was hospitalized for three weeks. Everyone I knew must've believed I was mentally ill because I wasn't allowed to visit him. Friends kept me informed of his condition, but one day I insisted on seeing him at the hospital. Normally, he was a chubby toddler but was thin and pale. I wondered, "Will I lose this child, too?"

Denny never technically deployed to Korea, as he was delayed in Oakland, California and the Red Cross took four long months to bring him home. I needed him and as a couple, we needed support. I wanted to have another baby and though my doctor advised against it, I got pregnant again. In fact, we had two more children, both girls. Though they were healthy, I lived with guilt and unanswered questions about Susan's death for many years. In fact, I received psychiatric counsel for more than 10 years.

When Denny was later deployed to Vietnam, I faced single parenting. When he was home, he was critical and verbally abusive. Many times, I felt like I was walking on glass. Altogether, we had 58 years of tumultuous marriage. I do remember one moment when Denny's heart softened. About 40 years after Susan died, we both visited her grave in Kansas, and we were kneeling, wind blowing, when he sobbed and we both wept over her short life. I know we both carried that burden for many years.

Though I'd been raised in the church and baptized at 10, we adhered to legalistic rules and I never experienced a personal relationship with God. Because of my pain, years passed before I sought Him or began to believe that He had not punished me and Denny for what happened. On a weekend retreat, I let go of the guilt and the notion that God had punished us by taking Susan from us. Finally, I understood my salvation wasn't based on good works but instead what had already been done for me at the cross.

The truth is, I never "lost" my baby. People say the worst things in times of grief. Things like, "Your baby is an angel in Heaven now." "God took her away because He needed her." I don't use those words with others who are suffering because I know that everything that happens is filtered through God. He allows things to happen and sometimes those events are unbearable, but He loves us and comforts us. He also puts people in our path like my psychologist, who encouraged me and helped me through my grief. Through the process, I learned to trust myself again and to trust God.

Grief & Gratitude

"Answer me when I call to you, my righteous God. Give me relief from my distress; have mercy on me and hear my prayer." (Psalm 4:1)

Prayer: Heavenly Father, thank You for not turning a deaf ear to me when I was scared and lost. Thank You for rescuing me from judgmental people and for new beginnings. Thank You for restoring my heart and my trust in You.

Linda

"Mom, I'm gay."

My son was 17 and I was in shock. I was hurt. Those words took me back to when he was in the second grade and I found him in my closet dressed in my clothes. I asked him what he was doing, and he could not express himself. At 17, he did. I rebuked his behavior in my heart, knowing his lifestyle was a sin but loving my son so much.

In many ways, I felt sorry for Hassan. I never married his father and he wasn't involved in his life. In fact, he never met his father until he was 22. He struggled in school and never got his diploma or GED. He couldn't hold a job down. Two months after he told me he was gay, we found out he was also HIV-positive.

I screamed, "Not my child! I can't believe it! Why, God? Please deliver him from this!" I was so hurt and so afraid. I had begged him to stop going out with men who were strange and dangerous, and as a single mom with four other children, I also had to think about his health care.

Just a few years prior, I had surrendered my life to Christ. I had another son by a man, and three daughters by a different father, and I was reaping many of the struggles that you would expect as a single mother. However, I began to live an abstinent life. I took my children to church and taught them Biblical principles. I prayed for them and I asked God to spare my oldest son's life. I begged him to repent and surrender his life to God. He ignored me, with dull eyes and no conviction.

I talked with my pastor and friends, who all encouraged me and continued to pray for Hassan. I knew I had to accept him. Not acceptance in the sense that my son should live a sinful life, but to accept my son and love him and accept that God can do His work in His time. I won't tell you that I am not fearful. Many times, when I don't hear from my son because his phone is cut off, I fear for his life.

Further, I fear for the men whose health and lives he may have affected.

I had so many dreams for my son when he was a little boy, but those dreams have been shattered. I pray that my son will surrender his life and his future to the Lord, because his salvation is even more important to me than his health. However, I trust my God, the One who saved me, the One who loves me, and the One who loved His own son so much that He allowed Him to go to the cross for me and all mankind.

Grief & Gratitude

"Peace I leave with you; my peace I give you. I do not give to you as the world gives. Do not let your hearts be troubled and do not be afraid." (John 14:27)

Prayer: Gracious Lord, I am distraught when my children are lost and on the wrong path. I trust You and I ask You to protect them and draw them to yourself. Please put people in their path who will direct them toward You.

Racquel

"I just want to see you smile again," my husband said.

On Mother's Day, we were reminiscing through photo albums, admiring our two children. I was trying to cover up my depression, which was not working very well. Over the course of just a few years, I'd spiraled out of control. My last straw was when Tristen was six, and his first grade teacher told us she could do nothing more for him. He would need a self-contained classroom to thrive. I was distraught and felt like a failure for not being able to "fix" Tristen.

Tristen is 10 now and when he was born, he was a healthy six pound 13-ounce baby. He developed on a normal track for about 18 months before I noticed that he was struggling. I am an occupational therapist by profession, mostly with adult patients, so I have a little training with children. However, when I began to see that my son was falling behind socially and later, academically, I mentioned my concerns to my husband. At first, he said I might be overthinking things, but later he noticed what I'd observed. At age six, everything came to a head. I was searching everywhere for answers and help, and did not know what we could do for sweet Tristen. By then, we also had a daughter though I wasn't enjoying being a parent very much. I isolated myself and knew not where to go.

I was raised a Catholic but at a young age, I never felt that I had a relationship with God. God was all about a religion for me. My sister, who lives nearby, had visited a large thriving church and invited me to go one Sunday. I decided to give the church a try, and for the first time, I found a release and became a Christ follower. My entire life changed forever. Most importantly, God revealed to me three things:

- I was not by myself and I did not have to solve things alone.

- I didn't need to "fix" Tristen. Though I felt a burden, God told me he was not broken.

- God has a plan for Tristen's life, and even at 10, He loves him and Tristen will be in Heaven one day.

These revelations were so freeing for me! At the same time, I discovered that this new church had several small groups, but when I inquired whether they might have a support group for moms of special needs children, I was told no. I was encouraged to start one myself.

Now, I'm shy and have never considered myself a leader, but through prayer and support, God began to direct my path. At first, I started and advertised a support group off campus. No one showed for the first four or five months and I was disappointed. Still, I didn't worry, and I trusted God that He would bring the right people in His timing. The next semester, we held the group on the church campus and three moms came at first. Slowly, we invited other moms from the community. Week by week, we shared ideas, gave each other support, and we continued to blossom. Special needs children can put a strain on the whole family, we agreed.

At one meeting, a mom who is a lawyer by profession, suggested we might start up a nonprofit and expand our model to the community. Again, I wasn't the most qualified person to lead it, but through encouragement, we formed a board of directors and are in the process of launching "Ray of Hope Support Network."

The reason for the name Ray of Hope is that I have a strong connection with rays. Even as a child, during or after a storm, I'd stare at the sky and still see one ray of sunshine that I could hold on to. As an adult, I know that no matter what storm I am facing personally, like the one we faced with Tristen, I can hold on to the promises of God and never give up hope. Even in the worst of times, the rays are still there. I recognize that each of the moms, like me, will grieve a piece of what could have been in regards to their children. I did too. What I once thought I could "fix," I realize now I can't. I don't need to fix him and I don't fight his disability, but I accept him. I trust God more than ever, and perhaps my precious son drew me to that place.

Grief & Gratitude

"May the God of hope fill you with all joy and peace as you trust in him, so that you may overflow with hope by the power of the Holy Spirit." (Romans 15:13)

Prayer: Father, when I am in the midst of a storm, draw me near so that I can see a ray of your light again and be full of hope again.

P atti

"Mom, can you send me some money?"

"Ben, you know I can't do that, but I want you to know I love you and God loves you."

My son, 32, was in ICU, and was told that if he left, he would lose his foot and die. Ben is diabetic, bipolar, and homeless. He's addicted to OxyContin, has been to rehab before, and rejects any type of help. He has no identification on him, and he has been arrested 10 times. I'm constantly anxious, waiting for a call. I love my son but I've learned the only thing I can do is pray for him.

Ben was a young boy with juvenile diabetes when he started smoking pot with his friends. Refusing to take his insulin complicated his health, coupled with his mental illness. We sent him to special schools, sought counseling, and put our hope in the "system," which let us down. By the time Ben graduated from high school, he left home and spiraled. He was working in construction when a garage wall fell on him, breaking several bones.

He was in a physical rehabilitation program when he became addicted to painkillers. He seemed stable at times, until something would trigger him and he worsened. Ben lived with us for a while during his adulthood, until we discovered he was stealing from us. With no regard for us, my husband became very angry and asked him to leave. After he left, if Ben needed money, he would call us, but I had to decline his request. As a mother, that was difficult but I began to learn about setting boundaries.

As a Catholic, I attended mass regularly and prayed for my son. One day, I met a woman who enlightened me by introducing me to the Holy Spirit and educating me about God. I began to pray in a different way than ever before. I asked the Holy Spirit to guide my words toward Ben so that they were not judgmental, but loving and firm. Soon thereafter, I was diagnosed with stomach cancer.

The cancer lasted five years and I went through chemotherapy treatments for 24 weeks. When I would lie down in my recliner, I would pray or read the Bible and became more intimate with God. I never blamed Him for my cancer or for my son's issues. God took away my fears and comforted me. I was in remission for a while, while my doctors tried new drugs and within 12 weeks, I was cancer-free. I was granted a miracle, and I rejoiced.

In the past year, I've become involved with a homeless ministry through a women's group at church. The ministry provides umbrellas and food to homeless people in our area, and I am free to talk with them, give hugs, or share Christ with them. I've discovered that this ministers to me! I see Ben's eyes in these people and I am comforted. I hear their stories and I understand how Ben's life must be.

This past Thanksgiving, when he was in ICU, was the last time I talked to my son. His condition filled me with anxiety. Thankfully, God gets me through the dark times and fills me with His peace. I still pray and release Ben to God. With Him, I know all things are possible.

Grief & Gratitude

"Dear children, let us not love with words or speech but with actions and in truth." (1 John 3:18)

Prayer: Gracious God, I am speechless when I observe how You work your miracles. I can't thank You enough for your mercy on me and on my child, when I can do nothing for him. Help me to love him and to love others by my actions, just as You do.

Trudi

"I know your passion for kids and you're probably going to be given a whole household of them. Those whose parents are not in Heaven with them."

My 42-year-old son, Ryan, was asleep so I used that time to express myself to him. Strange as this may sound, I felt that the pieces of the puzzle were coming together and it was prime time for God to take my son home. He'd been diagnosed a few months before but we were preparing ourselves.

Though his marriage had faltered even his wife agreed to talk to him by phone, showing appreciation for the things he'd done for her. I was disappointed in her earlier when she said she just wanted to remember him "the way he was before the cancer." However, I could also see how God was reconciling that in His own special way. After days of the hospice staff coming by and wondering myself how he could still be holding on, I realized that he was waiting on that last piece of the puzzle before taking his last breath. When he did, I knew he was safely tucked in for the night with the Lord, and he was cheering us all on.

Ryan was my first born and while he was young, he clashed with his father. My husband was not a Christian at the time, and my two sons had to make their own faith choice. Ryan made the choice to follow Christ and became a leader in his junior year of high school. Aside from going to school he worked at a local burger place, as a waiter in a seafood restaurant, and later as a cook.

He had many talents, but Ryan chose painting as a profession and made a living at it. He was also quite unique in that he maintained his sexual abstinence until he was married. He eventually married and wanted children, but that did not happen. His wife and he drifted apart and had agreed to divorced, but Ryan became a wonderful uncle to his two nieces and a nephew. I remember how he loved researching new games, and introducing them to us on Christmas Eve. He was the life of the party and very selfless.

In May of 2015 at midnight, I received a phone call from a friend of Ryan's, telling me that she was with him at the emergency room and that the medical team needed the next of kin. They found a brain tumor and wanted to start surgery the next day. He'd previously had some symptoms when he visited a walk-in clinic for a spot on his back. However, due to his finances, he declined any biopsy or treatment. Unfortunately, the spot on his back spread to his brain and we faced cancer.

The surgery went well and doctors suggested that he have radiation. Ryan had seen my husband after radiation treatments for his own throat cancer years before, and Ryan did not want to go through it. Shortly thereafter, Ryan lost the use of his left side. Eventually, he did do some treatments which allowed him to walk again, but by October, he had worsened.

During this time, though I was grieving, I realized Ryan had a win-win situation. If he lived, we would have him for longer. If he died, he would go to Heaven and have full wholeness for eternity. Because of my faith and full trust in God, I could sacrifice my own desires and believe that losing him was all part of God's timing and plan. In fact, I'm not sure I "lost" as much as others had when Ryan passed.

Though I did see him occasionally as an adult living on his own, I did not see him as often or consistently as the people for whom he painted. As a mom, I think perhaps it's an advantage to live further from your child because when they are gone, the pain doesn't hurt quite as much. Don't get me wrong, I still have felt the "ambush" at times – usually on his birthday or a holiday or anniversary date. I think that is normal with grief.

In fact, I decided to join a grief group, along with Ryan's friend, and that helped me. People in the group shared their experiences and different aspects of grief, and we realized what we have in common.

Now I tell people who are facing a loss that no matter what, God is good and you can trust Him. The year he died I focused on one word for that whole year. My word was TRUST. Because I know that God is sovereign in all His ways, I trust Him. He's got us covered.

Grief & Gratitude

"Be joyful in hope, patient in affliction, faithful in prayer." (Romans 12:12)

Prayer: Father, I am grateful that You understand more than anyone what it's like to lose a son. You willingly gave your son so that I could have abundant life and I thank You for that gift. Though difficult at times to grasp my loss, I trust that You ordered every minute of his life and I thank You for giving him to me for the years that You did. I am so grateful he gets to spend eternity with you.

Elizabeth

"Three legs." I wondered what that meant. Maybe I was woozy from the sedation.

As a single mom, I worked all day and attended college at night. One night after class, a man who was high on drugs approached me wanting sex, and when I refused he put a knife to my toddler's throat, who was with me in my car. Terrified and alone, in a matter of minutes I was the victim of sexual assault.

I went home and after putting my baby to bed, I took a very long shower. I didn't call the police to report the rape because I'd had a friend who experienced the same ordeal and received no support. Still, I felt traumatized and alone.

In December, during Christmas break, I felt sick and skipped a period. January came and when I still felt ill, I took a pregnancy test which was positive. I didn't receive any counsel and I had no family support. I was all alone. I found a woman to take me to the abortion clinic. That was February third. I don't remember much about the procedure other than hearing the nurse and those haunting words. "Three legs." Clearly, she must've been new or didn't know the proper code and protocol to use.

Two months later I was still nauseous. When I went to see my doctor, I was told that the abortion was incomplete and that I was still carrying a partial baby. They would need to do a D&C immediately. Traumatized by the rape itself, the abortion procedure, and now a D&C, I was in shock. Again, I was all alone.

Unfortunately, no amount of work or academics or relationships could fill the void of an abortion. Approximately ten years passed before I faced the pain of what I did. Thankfully, I was going to a church in Tennessee and I found a post-abortion counseling group. That group was led by a woman who was post-abortive herself, has training, and helps each woman in the group come to a place of healing. During the class, we each shared our experiences and wrote a letter to ourselves.

We sought forgiveness and we prayed for our lost children. We even had a memorial service and named our children, so I chose Sarah and Joshua. They both were Biblical names and fairly common.

A few months after the group ended, I began teaching swim classes to young children. At the time, I had a preschool aged child who came to class with her mother. Normally, we held a small graduation ceremony when the children had completed their swim lessons for the season, but this child, named Sarah, could not attend. To accept her certificate, her father took her place.

When I first saw him, I didn't recognize him. I had matured in my Christian faith and prayed to God to prepare my heart and to help me forgive the man who raped me. Imagine my shock when this man recognized me, years later, and told me that he too had repented, prayed for forgiveness, and asked God to reveal his victim to him. He asked for my forgiveness which I granted, but never told him of the child or the abortion. I didn't know what good could come of that. He was a chaplain in the Army and a very kind man. I learned later that he became a well-known pastor and speaker.

You don't realize what effects rape and abortion do to your self-esteem. I questioned my worth and had difficulty later with intimacy within a marriage. Triggers such as anniversary dates of the abortion or seeing adult children affected me, and affect others. I am grateful that God eventually healed me and delivered me from my shame.

I was blessed with having other children for which I am grateful, and I've had the opportunity to speak and give my testimony at women's groups. I tell women who are walking around carrying guilt and shame that until they let go and allow God to heal them, they can't experience the abundance and grace He gives. I wish that more churches would speak about abortion without judgment or stigma and offer supportive groups, just as they do for divorce or bereavement. Just like homeless people or prisoners, women in unplanned pregnancies are lost and need to be loved. I am grateful for God's overflowing grace and abundant love.

Grief & Gratitude

"For his anger lasts only a moment, but his favor lasts a lifetime; weeping may stay for the night, but rejoicing comes in the morning." (Psalm 30:5)

Prayer: Messiah, I am so grateful that You took what was meant for evil and You made it good. You turned my ashes to beauty. You carried me through the pain and You supernaturally gave me a heart of forgiveness. Thank You for loving me, for your mercy, and for being my Savior.

Julie

"Please, you don't have to do this...come closer, and let me help you."

I was driving across the Centennial Bridge from Missouri to Kansas when I stopped my car, 30 years old and ready to end my life. I wasn't even sure what was happening to me, but something came over me that put me over the edge. Thankfully, I didn't jump over the edge. A man who was on that bridge came over gently, took my hand, and drove me to a hospital. After years of intense counseling, I am convinced that man was an angel that God sent to me.

I wasn't so sure that God cared or even knew what was happening to me when I was a young girl. Beginning at age of seven, my oldest brother sexually molested and abused me. Because our family raised, boarded and trained dogs, my parents were very busy and expected us to do all the chores. My sister and I were not close and to my knowledge, she was not molested. My younger brother, Jimmy, was my protector when no one else was.

"What are you doing? Get off her!" yelled my brother Jimmy.

My older brother would lock me in a dog crate or in our station wagon outside so that the family would not notice what he was doing to me. This time, Jimmy saw. He was furious and confronted him but never told our parents. I never told my parents, teachers, or friends out of fear and shame. I dated a young man in high school – a sweet, gentle guy who I later moved to Texas with, but I never told him either. I wanted to marry him but I got homesick and left, one of the greatest regrets of my life. Back at home, I tried to rebuild my life, going to school and opening an interior design store.

Years later, I met and married an ex-marine, very macho and proud. When I told him of my sexual abuse, he said, "Oh, grow up. Just suck it up, you're okay." As if forgetting what happened to me was that easy. We had two sons together and his job took him to Afghanistan.

After some time working there, he decided he wanted nothing to do with me or our kids. I was heartbroken. I wondered, "Where are you God?! Don't you care about me?"

I knew about God because of my grandmother. She took us to the Episcopal church and I was confirmed at 11 or 12 years old. During the years of my abuse, I prayed for it to stop but it didn't. I didn't understand why and I felt abandoned by God. Then, I lost six family members in a row.

At one of their funerals, on a nasty rainy day, our family was sitting in the church pew. I was thinking how doomed we were, how terrible my life was. Then remarkably a light came through the church window and shined on the one pew where we sat. I thought, "Wow, God, you really are here and you do care." That was the first time I could see any light in my dark world.

You see, my heavenly Father was the only person I could trust other than my brother Jimmy. When I tried to tell my mother about the rape, she said, "Well don't tell your father, he'll have a heart attack." I was devastated. That was not the answer I wanted or needed. She never asked me how I was doing emotionally. At that moment, I realized just how dysfunctional my family was. No child should ever be put in the position I was. My innocence was robbed. My marriage was horribly affected. I attempted suicide three times.

If not for God and a caring counselor for the past 16 years, I'd have been paralyzed. In fact, I broke my back and went on disability, with horrible pain. I decided then that I might be broken, but I would not allow my brother to ruin my life or Satan to destroy me. I was not and am not judge, jury and executioner but he must face his Maker one day.

Both of my parents are gone. My abusive brother still lives nearby and I am learning to forgive. My protective brother rejected God, due to our abuse, but through prayers and my encouragement, he's now a seeker. My counselor often talks with me about forgiveness, and I realize I must do that to be free. I wear an armband that reminds me I can bear all things. I am more than a conqueror. I am not beaten down and I am not destroyed. I have purpose and now I can help others.

Grief & Gratitude

"I can do all things through Him who gives me strength." (Philippians 4:13)

Prayer: Jesus, I am alive because You gave me the strength to carry on. I am so grateful that You loved me in the midst of my pain and You continue to hold me in your loving care.

Ellen

"Everyone's dead!" I screamed to the scuba instructor. All I saw were floating bodies.

"No, they're not dead. Everyone is breathing. Are you okay?" he asked.

I was not okay by any stretch. That was the first trigger of many and the beginning of the nightmares, sometimes four or five times a night, the beginning of my panic attacks and the beginning of my depression. Those episodes were the start of my cry for help.

My husband and I were stationed in Guam with a one-year-old baby when I told him I had to return home to the U.S. If not, I would die. I told him my soul was for sale, a battle between good and evil. He knew that I was experiencing nightmares and flashbacks, but he didn't know I had suicidal thoughts at times. I wanted to see my mother, and I wanted to get to a hospital as fast as I could. My husband was devastated but understood how serious my mental state was.

When I arrived home, I convinced my mom that I needed psychiatric care NOW. I was full of rage and needed deliverance. Once admitted to the hospital, I spent the first three days sleeping and was given an anti-depressant drug. The psychiatrist asked me, "Did anyone ever hurt you as a child?"

As I slowly revealed to her, I was ritually and sexually abused by a satanic cult member, beginning at age seven. My older brother had been involved in what I assume was a drug deal gone bad and he "sold" me to his dealer. The man was about 19, an addict and a pedophile. He threatened me and another brother who was "sold," that he would kill our parents and other siblings if we told anyone.

The abuse took place in an otherwise "normal" neighborhood in the 1970's, when parents allowed their children to play outside all day, and before we knew anything about "stranger danger." Once I told my mother what had occurred, she immediately believed me and

119

understood better why my siblings were so dysfunctional. She grieved with me over the loss of my innocence, my childhood, and my ability to function normally as an adult. Since then, I've severed ties with most of my siblings except my younger brother, who was in private child care at the time.

For four brutal years of my childhood, I thought I was dying a slow death by a million cuts. Though I went to church and knew God loved me, I was taught by the cult leader to believe that God was not real, that I was unworthy, and that I was a child of Satan. I became a marionette for this evil man. Though I was tortured, I tried to wear a "normal" face in public. He told me that the only reason he would not kill me was that I was birthed and named outside of the cult. That is sadly not the case for young, female children that are birthed and tortured within.

The word *abuse* is not an accurate description of what I witnessed or endured. I used what therapists call "disassociation" so I could cope with what was happening to me. I thought I would die as a child so during these rituals, I would daydream about places where I wanted to go, that were safe and allowed me to do childlike things. All the time, I prayed to God to save me and promised Him that if He did, I would follow and serve Him.

Finally, my family and I moved away to another state. I spent my middle and high school years doing average teenage things. I got good grades, dated, was social, and was driven to graduate. I went to college and earned two degrees. I was drawn to my husband because he was so fun and caring and came from a "normal" family. He was my warrior. Many nights when I would have nightmares and wake up screaming, he would hold me, saying, "I will never harm you. God has already won the battle. He has your soul."

The demonic detoxing was evident. Over the years, I saw several therapists who I later learned were all Christians. No doubt they were praying for me. Through some wonderful therapy methods and sessions, I learned to release those horrific memories. Before that, I would often go into a dark abyss when I couldn't endure the pain.

As I matured, I wanted to go deeper with Jesus. I joined every Bible study offered by any church. I dug deep into scripture, and though the women in the groups did not know my story, I believe they could see my scars. My heart was as hard as stone until God began to soften it. He was the only one who could heal me.

One of the worst things I remember about my experience with the abusive cult was seeing two young girls with big dark eyes, who could not talk. They were more like animals than humans and I thought they might try and bite me if I spoke. I knew that they'd been born into this cult and were not named, so they could be used for pleasure and pain. Still, I thought this to myself:

"I don't know your names, but God does. You didn't have a chance in this world and you will probably not survive before I am back here again. But God loves you and created you and you will be safe when you are in Heaven with Him. Your names are written in His book. I will remember you. I promise I will never forget you."

I am so grateful that God did not forget me or forsake me. He was with me throughout my horrible journey to Hell and back and as I promised, I serve Him today. I am a therapist who works with girls who were trafficked and from broken dysfunctional homes. Jesus touched my heart and made me whole again. I have come full circle. I am redeemed.

When you choose to walk the Christian path, you pick up your cross and I am living proof of that. However, the cross that I go to is not the typical one you picture. When I am with Christ, I am at the foot of a blood-stained cross, with a suffering, bleeding Jesus. I know He experienced pain and suffering like I did, and that He loves me so much that He claimed me at birth for His own. Because of that love, I can spend eternity with Him in Heaven and not in Hell.

Grief & Gratitude

"For just as we share abundantly in the sufferings of Christ, so also our comfort abounds through Christ." (2 Corinthians 1:5)

Prayer: Dear Jesus, I am so grateful that You understand my suffering and You have been with me all along. You, too, suffered and went to the cross for my sins to save me from the abyss of Hell. I am eternally grateful that You bought me with a price and adopted me as your child. Thank You for taking my place. Thank You for healing. You are my Rock and my Redeemer.

About Melissa

Melissa Jansen is a life coach, conference speaker, and first-time author. Melissa lived all over the U.S. before graduating from the University of Kansas with a bachelor's degree in Education. She attended several graduate schools and seminary, and received her advanced certification in life coaching through the International Board of Christian Care (IBCC), an affiliate of the American Association of Christian Counselors.

Melissa is the founder and owner of Next Steps Life Coaching, where she specializes in Grief, Relationship/Marriage, and Life Purpose Coaching. She currently resides in Florida with her husband and loves the beach, theatre, and traveling. She is passionate about helping people identify issues, set goals, overcome obstacles, and reach their full potential.

Melissa would love to connect with you!

Website: http://www.melissamjansen.com/

Email: mmjansen61@gmail.com

Facebook: https://www.facebook.com/melissa.m.jansen

LinkedIn: https://www.linkedin.com/in/melissa-jansen-8aa97914/

Instagram: mmjansen61

Made in the USA
Columbia, SC
03 July 2017